T. P. (Tarleton Perry) Crawford

The Patriarchal dDynasties from Adam to Abraham

Shown to Cover 10,500 Years, and the Highest Human Life Only 187

T. P. (Tarleton Perry) Crawford

The Patriarchal dDynasties from Adam to Abraham
Shown to Cover 10,500 Years, and the Highest Human Life Only 187

ISBN/EAN: 9783337157647

Printed in Europe, USA, Canada, Australia, Japan

Cover: Foto ©Lupo / pixelio.de

More available books at **www.hansebooks.com**

THE
Patriarchal Dynasties

FROM

ADAM TO ABRAHAM,

SHOWN TO COVER 10,500 YEARS, AND THE
HIGHEST HUMAN LIFE ONLY 187.

BY

Rev. T. P. CRAWFORD,

OF TUNG CHOW, CHINA.

RICHMOND, VA.:
JOSIAH RYLAND & CO., 913 MAIN STREET,
1877.

CONTENTS.

	PAGE.
INTRODUCTION, ...	5

CHAPTER I.
The Length of Life according to the Antediluvian Table of Genesis; Average age, 120 years, ... 11

CHAPTER II.
The Length of Life according to the Postdiluvian Table; Average Age, 128 years, ... 36

CHAPTER III.
Adam, at his Death, appointed Seth his Spiritual Successor and Representative, ... 45

CHAPTER IV.
The Adamic Family and Government Reconstructed, . . 54

CHAPTER V.
The House of Adam continued 800 years after the Death of Adam, its Founder; so of the other Patriarchal Houses to Abraham; the whole equal to 10,500 years, . . 70

CHAPTER VI.

The Dynastic Scheme of Scripture Chronology in harmony with Reason, ... 93

CHAPTER VII.

The Dynastic Theory of Interpreting the Tables in the Fifth and Eleventh Chapters of Genesis, or a Long Chronology, in harmony with the General Teachings of the Bible, ... 100

CHAPTER VIII.

Corroborated by History, ... 124

CHAPTER IX.

By Science, Tradition, and Mythology, ... 135

APPENDIX.

Chinese Uranography; Astronomy of the Babylonians; A Chronological Table by different authors; Dates at which various Eras begin, ... 151

NOTE.

The author of this work being resident in China, the Publishers have been obliged to pass it through the press without affording him an opportunity for its final revision. While great care has been exercised to secure accuracy, yet among the numerous references to Chinese ancient history, it is probable that the critical reader may find several inaccuracies, more especially in proper names.

INTRODUCTION.

THE term of man's existence on the earth is the great question of the age. Astronomy and Geology have of late wonderfully enlarged our conceptions of time and space. Under their inspiration, the horizon has expanded into a boundless universe, and the "six days of creation," into as many vast periods of duration.

Ethnology, philology, and other kindred studies, have, in like manner, so extended the bounds of human history as to overthrow all our systems of chronology, and leave the public mind without landmarks, or reliable dates for the ages prior to the birth of Abraham. Divines, as well as scientific men, constantly feel the need of more time in which to account for the many evidences of high antiquity arresting their attention than the Hebrew Scriptures, or even the Septuagint version of them, seem to furnish.

On account of the painful state of doubt and uncertainty which now prevails on the subject, every sincere effort to discover the truth, to remove the embarrassment that increasing wisdom has produced, and bring faith, reason and facts into harmony, will be welcomed by all honest minds, no matter by whom it may be made, or from what source the desired information may be drawn.

The difficulty, as I shall endeavor to show, is apparent rather than real, having grown out of a general misunderstanding of the tabulated names and dates recorded in the fifth and eleventh chapters of the Book of Genesis.

My attention was first drawn to this fact, over three years ago, while preparing an "Epitome of Ancient History," in the Chinese language. This language, which I have now been using nearly a quarter of a century, presents many thoughts and expressions in striking resemblance to those of the ancient Hebrew. Influenced by this resemblance and a casual remark of an ordinary man, I discovered the key, as I confidently believe, with which to

INTRODUCTION. 7

unlock the casket, and bring to light the true ages of the patriarchs, and the system of chronology contained in those important chapters. I shall, therefore, attempt, in the present work, to establish the two following propositions:

I.

That the antediluvian patriarchs did not live as individual men to the marvelous length of over eight and nine hundred years, but on an average only one hundred and twenty, and the postdiluvians one hundred and twenty-eight.

II.

That the two tables of Genesis present, in regular succession, nineteen patriarchal houses, dynasties, or governments, covering a term of, at least, ten thousand five hundred years duration. Or thus:

From Adam to the flood,	7,737 years.
" the flood to the birth of Abraham,	2,763 "
	10,500
" the birth of Abraham to Christ,	2,000
	12,500
" Christ to the present time,	1,876
Making a sum total of	14,376

for the existence of man on the earth, beginning with Adam, the father of Seth, instead of only six or seven thousand, as generally supposed.

I am fully aware of the boldness of these propositions, and also of the mighty consequences involved in their establishment. I know they imply a "change of base," among the various learned combatants now in the field, the modification of many opinions, the fall of many theories, the revision of many books, and liberty for all to believe both in the Bible and in modern discoveries. The field is a very wide one, and I shall not attempt to give all the steps by which my present convictions have been reached, but only a general outline of the proofs and arguments on which they rest, and leave the result to the judgment of others, in the hope that all false notions as to the length of human life in primitive times may be corrected, and a true system of chronology spring from my humble efforts.

TUNG CHOW, *Feb.*, 1876.

THE PATRIARCHAL DYNASTIES

FROM

ADAM TO ABRAHAM.

PROPOSITION FIRST.

The antediluvian patriarchs did not live, as individual men, to the marvelous age of over eight and nine hundred years; but, on an average, only one hundred and twenty; and the postdiluvians, one hundred and twenty eight.

PROPOSITION SECOND.

The two tables of Genesis present a regular succession of nineteen houses, dynasties, or governments, covering a term of at least ten thousand five hundred years.

CHAPTER I.

THE LENGTH OF LIFE ACCORDING TO THE ANTEDILUVIAN TABLE.

THE human mind naturally arranges all objects and events according to their relations to each other in time and space. The multiplication of the former requires a corresponding extension of the latter. During the last half century our knowledge of the facts pertaining to the past has greatly increased; hence the strong desire for a more extended system of chronology than any of those heretofore received. Scholars of various schools have searched most earnestly in every direction for reliable data on which to construct it, except the one where it is found—the tabulated names and dates in the fifth and eleventh chapters of Genesis. These, beginning with the head of the race, continue the succession of patriarchal governments, along the chosen line of Seth, through the primitive ages of the world down to the birth of Abraham, about 2000 B. C. Then the detailed history of himself and posterity opens, and dates become more satisfactory. The first or antediluvian table reads, according to our English translation and punctuation, as follows:

1. "And Adam lived 130 years, and begat *a son* in his own likeness, after his image; and called his name Seth: And the days of Adam after he begat Seth were 800 years: and he begat sons and daughters: And all the days that Adam lived were 930 years; and he died.
2. And Seth lived 105 years, and begat Enos: And Seth lived after he begat Enos 807 years, and begat sons and daughters: And all the days of Seth were 912 years; and he died.
3. And Enos lived 90 years, and begat Cainan: And Enos lived after he begat Cainan 815 years, and begat sons and daughters: And all the days of Enos were 905 years: and he died.
4. And Cainan lived 70 years, and begat Mahalaleel: And Cainan lived after he begat Mahalaleel 840 years, and begat sons and daughters: And all the days of Cainan were 910 years: and he died.
5. And Mahalaleel lived 65 years, and begat Jared: And Mahalaleel lived after he begat Jared 830 years, and begat sons and daughters: And all the days of Mahalaleel were 895 years: and he died.
6. And Jared lived 162 years, and he begat Enoch: And Jared lived after he begat Enoch 800 years,

and begat sons and daughters: And all the days of Jared were 962 years: and he died.

7. And Enoch lived 65 years, and begat Methuselah: And Enoch walked with God after he begat Methuselah 300 years, and begat sons and daughters: And all the days of Enoch were 365 years: And Enoch walked with God: and he was not; for God took him.

8. And Methuselah lived 187 years, and begat Lamech: And Methuselah lived after he begat Lamech 782 years, and begat sons and daughters: And all the days of Methuselah were 969 years: and he died.

9. And Lamech lived 182 years, and begat a son: And he called his name Noah, saying this same shall comfort us concerning our work and toil of our hands, because of the ground which the Lord hath cursed. And Lamech lived after he begat Noah 595 years, and begat sons and daughters: And all the days of Lamech were 777 years: and he died.

10. And Noah was 500 years old: and Noah begat Shem, Ham, and Japheth."

The above table, as is well known, has come down to us through the medium of the Hebrew language. The author is unknown, but it bears on its very face all the marks of historic verity, and has always commanded the highest respect. It is, even in its present form, confessedly a most ancient document. The materials from which it was composed must have been taken from antediluvian records—most probably by some one living in the five hundredth year of Noah, the point of time where it closes. That it was brought by Abraham into Canaan, subsequently passed through the hands of Moses and Aaron, received their sanction and translation into the then living Hebrew, is, to my mind, the most probable of all suppositions. The ages of which it treats being so remote, the words so few, archaic, and comprehensive, it becomes necessary for us of these modern days to study its import with the minutest attention, and by the light of all the learning, sacred and scientific, now in our possession. We enter upon the investigation with the firm conviction that its statements harmonize with established facts, and the invariable laws of nature.

In the first place, I would call the attention of the reader to the fact that the several sentences composing each of the paragraphs above quoted are, in the original text, all of the same kind, all equally complete and independent, all beginning with the conjunction " and," all wanting the nominative pronoun "he," and all but the last requiring the same pause, and the same punctuation mark,—in English, the colon or semi-colon. As the English language requires the nominative to be expressed before the leading verb in every such independent sentence, its omission here, in any case, will produce confusion as to the time and connection of the events recorded. Unfortunately, the translators of our Bible have, apparently without reason or discrimination, inserted the "he," in some places and left it out in others. The punctuation is also in the same unsatisfactory condition.

Thus they have, by uniting certain sentences too closely to the preceding ones, unintentionally encouraged false notions, both as to the chronology of the world, and the length of human life in its primitive ages. In this way the inspired document is made to speak contrary to the intention of its author, and becomes responsible for the most remarkable statements. For instance, a patriarch is not only made to live nearly a thousand years, but in one case he begat a son instead of dying, and in the next, he begat "sons and daughters," after he is dead. This latter absurdity shows plainly that the sentences are all complete and independent of each other. So far as this particular point is concerned, the first paragraph in the table should be rendered and punctuated in the following manner: "And Adam lived 139 years; And he begat *a son* in his *own* likeness, after his image; And he called his name Seth; And the days of Adam after begetting Seth were 800 years; And he begat sons and daughters; And all the days that Adam lived were 930 years; And he died."

Now, let us carefully study every thing in this leading paragraph, taking it up sentence by sentence. As it is the model one, its import will be substantially that of all the rest; and therefore it will not be necessary to attend particularly to them.

The key to the whole question under discussion may be found in the first sentence of each paragraph; as, "Adam lived 130 years," "Seth lived 105 years," etc. It is this. These figures mark the length of their individual lives, and not the time when their sons were born, as generally understood. To make this assertion good is the task now before us.

On the groundless assumption that they are birth dates has been based all the short and unsatisfactory theories as to the age of the human race, together with the absurd popular belief in the supernatural longevity of the ancient patriarchs. Divines, infidels, and scholars of every grade, alike taking this for granted, have, one after another, fallen into the same ditch, and also into endless controversies injurious to the common cause of truth. Some receiving the Bible with this understanding, reject the teachings of history and science as to those points; while others, receiving these, reject the Bible, as if it were responsible for interpretations, or for the difficulties growing out of them. I here take occasion to enter an earnest protest against the course of both these parties, and to urge every one to examine the subject for himself with a mind free from all such prejudices. The testimony of no one of these three witnesses can be rejected by us with impunity.

That my present understanding of the phrase "Adam lived 130 years" is correct—meaning he died at that time—may be shown by the following facts and arguments:

I. The Hebrew Scriptures never employ this kind of phraseology, or the verb "*lived*" with definite numbers, to indicate the age of a man at the birth of a son; but they invariably say, such an one *was a son of* blank years, *when* his son was born unto him, or some other event took place. The Hebrew, like all other languages, has its set forms of expression for turning a point of time, as may be clearly seen from the specimen passages which I shall present below. For instance:

Gen. xxi. 5. "Abraham was a son of an hundred years *when* his son Isaac was born unto him." Or, as our received version renders it, "Abraham *was* an hundred years *old when* his son Isaac was born unto him."

Gen. xvi. 16. "Abraham was a son of four score and six years when Hagar bare Ishmael unto him."

Gen. xvii. 24. "And Abraham was a son of ninety and nine years when he was circumcised."

Gen. xxi. 4. "And he circumcised his son Isaac, being a son of eight days."

Gen. xvii. 25. "And Ishmael his son was a son of thirteen years when he was circumcised."

Gen. xii. 4. "And Abram was a son of seventy-five years when he departed out of Haran."

Gen. xxv. 20. "And Isaac was a son of forty years when he took Rebekah to wife."

Gen. xxvi. 34. "And Esau was a son of forty years when he took Judith to wife."

Gen. xxxvii. 2. "And Joseph, being a son of seventeen years, was feeding the flock with his brethren."

Gen. v. 32. "And Noah was a son of five hundred years," (when God commanded him to prepare an ark for the saving of his house. See Gen. vi. 9–

19. Also, Heb. xi. 7; 1 Peter iii. 20.) "And Noah begat Shem, Ham, and Japheth." The generic and specific manner of using proper names will be discussed in another place.

Gen. vii. 6. "And Noah was a son of six hundred years when the flood of waters was upon the earth."

Gen. xi. 10. "And Shem was a son of an hundred years (when the flood began.) And he begat Arphaxad two years after the flood."

Lev. ix. 3. " Lambs and calves are sons of a year when they are taken for sacrifice."

Josh. xiv. 7. Caleb said, "A son of forty years was I, when Moses the servant of the Lord sent me to Cadesh-barnea to espy out the land."

1 Kings xiv. 21. "Rehoboam was a son of forty-one years when he began to reign."

1 Kings xxii 42. "Jehoshaphat was a son of thirty-five years when he began to reign," &c., &c.

Any one can readily see how awkward it would sound to say, Isaac lived forty years, and took Rebecca to wife; or, Jehosaphat lived thirty-five years, and began to reign; he lived thirty years and wrote a book, and the like. Many other passages can be brought forward to show that such is the phraseology constantly employed in the Old Testament to express the age of a man at the birth of a son, or the occurrence of some other event. The equivalents of our neuter verb *was*, and the adjective *old* occur in the first member of the sentence, with the adverb *when* in the second, in such cases.

To this rule I have not been able to find a single exception; and, therefore, to make the received interpretation of the text under consideration correct, it should read: "Adam was an hundred and thirty years old when his son was born unto him." Or, "Seth was an hundred and five years old when Enos was born."

Perhaps it might be said, he was 130 years old when he begat a son; but it cannot be said he *lived* 130 years and begat a son, either in Hebrew or in any other language, living or dead, as far as I am able to judge. The Greek, Latin, German, French, English, and Chinese, all say a man was so many years old, or of such an age, when a son was born, or something else took place—no matter how the construction of the words may be varied, the verb "liveth" is never employed in this manner. Does it then, in the catalogues of Genesis alone, form an exception to a universal law of human speech. It cannot be so, it seems to me.

But this is not all. It ~~is~~ *lived* the very word by which the Hebrew Bible indicates the termination of a man's life, or of existence of some kind, as the following passages will make abundantly plain:

Gen. l. 22. "And Joseph *lived* an hundred and ten years"—a phrase exactly similar to the one, "And Adam lived an hundred and thirty years;" or, "Seth lived an hundred and five years," &c. Now, we know that Joseph died at that time; for it is so stated in the twenty-sixth verse below.

Gen. xxiii. 1. "And the years of the life of Sarah were an hundred and twenty and seven years; these were the years of the life of Sarah."

Gen. xxv. 7. "These are the days of the years of Abraham's life which he lived, an hundred three score and fifteen years."

Gen. xlvii. 28. "And Jacob lived in the land of Egypt seventeen years;" at which time we learn he died.

Gen. v. 5. "And all the days that Adam lived were nine hundred and thirty years." It matters not whether the name Adam has here a generic or a specific sense, the verb "lived," in either case, refers to the end of existence.

Gen. xi. 11. "And Shem lived after he begat Arphaxad five hundred years." Nothing is said of his death, or of any other of the postdiluvian patriarchs mentioned in the second table. If they did not die at the end of the time to which they are said to have lived, they would still be alive, and "begetting sons and daughters."

Gen. ix. 28. "And Noah lived after the flood three hundred and fifty years."

2 Kings xiv. 17. "And Amaziah lived after the death of Jehoash fifteen years."

Job xlii. 16. "After this, Job lived an hundred and forty years, and saw his sons, and his sons' sons, even four generations."

Now, if Job "*saw*" his sons and sons' sons of four generations, that were born at various times within the 140 years, and Adam's "sons and daughters" were "begotten" within the 800 years, as is universally understood, then Seth was also born at some unspecified point *within* the 130 years, and not at their close. The three sentences are of the very same kind, and the births cannot be placed first within and then without the given number, according to the reader's arbitrary pleasure; but they must all be construed alike.

Since, then, the "130 years" do not specify the time of Seth's birth, they must of necessity specify the time of Adam's death; for there is nothing else to which they can possibly refer.

If such be the nature of the language employed in the Tables, then the individual man called by the name of

			Heb. Text.			Sam. Text.
Adam	lived *as a man*,		130 years.	*As a chief*,		130 years.
Seth	"	"	105 "	"	"	105 "
Enos	"	"	90 "	"	"	90 "
Cainan	"	"	70 "	"	"	70 "
Mahalaleel	"	"	65 "	"	".	65 "
Jared	"	"	162 "	"	"	62 "
Enoch	"	"	65 "	"	"	65 "
Methuselah	"	"	187 "	"	"	67 "
Lamech	"	"	182 "	"	"	53 "
Noah (Estimated)	"		143 "	"	"	(143) "

Or, on an average, the term of 120 years, instead of over 800.

I might now consider the sense of the first sentence in the paragraph under discussion as established, and proceed to the next one; but, lest some of my readers, through the influence of long custom, may be hard to satisfy, I will add still further proofs and arguments in support of the above interpretation.

II. That the life of the antediluvian patriarchs was on an average only 120 years is substantially asserted in the third verse of the sixth chapter of Genesis itself. It reads thus: "And the Lord said, My

Spirit shall not always strive (dwell) with man, for that he also is flesh; yet his days *shall be* an hundred and twenty years."

In the first place, notice the connection in which these words stand. Second, that the verb "shall be," in our Bible, is not the future, but the past tense, in the original text. Third, that the last clause in the verse is not necessarily the words of the Lord, but rather those of the author himself, the statement of an historical fact.

The author, no matter who he was, writes like all other historians, and records only past events. He can make no assertion as to the future, except by quoting a prophecy already in existence. Having begun with the third verse of the fifth chapter to give a list of the successive houses from Adam in the line of Seth, he continues straight on, without breaking the thread or turning aside to mention other matters, till he brings it down to his own time in the five hundredth year of Noah's reign, or life, or whatever you may call it. The table being thus completed, the author then goes back to the beginning in the chapter below (verse 1 to 9,) and gives a very brief but graphic account of the times over which he had before rapidly passed, till he comes again to Noah, in the eighth verse, where he brings his history to a close. Commencing with the ninth verse, the succeeding portions of Genesis seem to have been taken from postdiluvian documents.

As the first eight verses throw a flood of light on the antediluvian period of the world, it will be necessary for us to dwell sufficiently long to show their bearing upon the question in hand.

The first and second verses read: "And it came to pass when MEN *began to multiply* on the face of the earth, and daughters were born unto them, that the sons of God saw the daughters of men that they were fair; and they took them wives of all which they chose." The epithet "sons of God," as I take it, designates the Sethites who, from the days of Enos, "called on the name of the Lord," and shows that they were a religious party. The statement here is to the effect that some of them at a very early day began to intermarry, apparently contrary to their law, with the ungodly, or another party, differing in some important sense from their own. This, the author means to say, was the beginning of that corruption of morals among the Sethites which brought on an apostasy from the simplicity of life, piety, and virtue that originally prevailed. This lapse or apostasy, according to certain Jewish and Arabian traditions, finally culminated in the days of Jared—about midway between Adam and Noah, and divides the whole into two distinct periods. The intermarriage-apostasy, or whatever it may be called, formed a distinct epoch in the history of those times.

The third verse reads: "And the Lord said, My Spirit shall not always dwell with man, for that he also is flesh." Now, to whom did the Lord say these words? Are they not the death sentence pronounced on Adam in chapter iii. 19, "For dust thou art, and unto dust shalt thou return?" The two passages are substantially the same in sense. The writer, having made this quotation as to the origin of the mortality of man, adds the clause, "Yet his days," or the average limit of his life, "has been an hundred and twenty years." But I shall suspend further comment on this last clause till through with the next verse, the first portion of which reads thus:

"The Nephilim, or great men, (not "giants," as in our Bible,*) were in the earth in those days,"—that is, the patriarchs whose names come first in the table lived in those early and purer days before the intermarrying with the daughters of men prevailed

---

* Giants are not *men*, but fabulous beings.

among them. They were great, I suppose, for their piety and virtues, rather than for their prowess, since they stand in immediate contrast with the Giborim, or "mighty men" of the latter period, as may be seen from these words: "And after that (time,) when the sons of God came in unto the daughters of men, and they bare sons unto them, the same became the Giborim, or mighty men, who of old were the *men* of renown."

Supposing that the writer does not turn aside to tell about giants, barbarians, or hobgoblins of any kind, but confines himself strictly to the line of discourse, and to those patriarchs whose names, ages, and governments he had recorded in the table above, then by the term "Nephilim," or the great men of the former period, he must refer to Adam, Seth, Enos, Cainan, and Mahalaleel; by the "Giborim," or mighty men of the latter period, to Jared, Enoch, Methusaleh, and Noah, or some such division of them.

Again, observe that the "120 years" in the third verse stand connected with these two past periods of time and these two classes of men, even the latter of whom had become the "men of old and renown," prior to the five hundredth year of Noah, or one hundred years before the flood. These figures, then, either give the general average age of the patriarchs themselves, or the common limit of human life in antediluvian days—most probably the former, but the latter view is equally available for my present purpose.

Historians are accustomed to mention, among other things, the average life of men in the times and nations of which they treat, and that such was the intention of the writer of this text, I have not the most distant doubt. Every other explanation which I have yet seen is wholly untenable. The first clause of the verse is certainly the words of the writer, the middle portion down to "flesh" as certainly those of the Lord, but whose are the last clause? They seem to me to be the words of the writer himself. If so, he states an historical fact, and they should be rendered in the past tense. The "and" of the first clause, then, should be taken in the sense of *though* answered by the "and" of the last in the sense of *yet*. Thus: "Though the Lord said, My spirit shall not always dwell with man, for that he is flesh (or mortal); yet his days have been 120 years."

Now, *vav conversive* used here refers back to the verb "said," which is the word of the writer; and if it converts his past tense into a future, it must also convert him from a historian into a prophet, which is not admissible. But take the clause, if you prefer, as the words of the Lord, and in the future tense, the result will be the same; for the question still remains, to whom did he address them, to Adam, or to Noah?

If to Adam, then they were quoted to show that such, from his time down to the five hundredth year of Noah, had been the average limit of man's life. This interpretation of the text corresponds with the proofs already brought forward to show the comparatively short lives of the antediluvian patriarchs, just as well as the other. For their average age as put down in the table is 120 years, and agrees with the words of the clause, whether those of the Lord, or those of the writer.

On the other hand, they could not have been spoken to Noah or any of his contemporaries; for they are in no way associated with his name or his times, but with the times "when men *began to multiply* upon the face of the earth." They stand prior to the days of the "giants," or rather the great men, whose sons "afterwards became the mighty men who *of old* were the men of renown." How, then, can they be made to jump over all these days and apply to Noah and the last hundred years before the flood? Such confusion in the order of language is not to be presumed. If they had been addressed to Noah, they would naturally be found recorded in connection with the seventh or thirteenth verse, instead of the third, as any one can see. As the record in the fifth chapter had been brought down to within one hundred years of the flood, how can the expression refer to that catastrophe? Could even those sinners get 120 years out of 100? Or, from what point are they to be calculated? The prevailing opinion that Noah was 120 years building the ark is without support; there being no such statement either in the Old or the New Testament.

Further, the language of the third verse, "My Spirit shall not always dwell with man, for that he is flesh," or mortal, is not applicable to the sudden destruction of the race in health and vigor by a deluge, but to death by the ordinary operations of nature. That such was the writer's meaning when he penned these words is most evident.

It would never have received any other explanation, if commentators had not first fallen into the error of supposing that the ancient patriarchs were a kind of giants, able to live a thousand years! Such ideas have happily had their day. By the way, the translators of our Bible have rendered several different Hebrew words by the term "giant!" It may be well for western people to know that the Chinese in common conversation indiscriminately apply the epithet *ta jin*, "big men," to persons of respectability, age, virtue, office, or unusual size.

Other desperate interpretations of the text are not worth refutation, and nothing more need be said under this head.

III. Outside of the tables, the meaning of which is now in dispute, there is not in all the Bible the most distant allusion to any such ages as eight and nine hundred years. The idea was not only unknown to Abraham, Isaac, and Moses; but there are passages inconsistent with the existence of such a belief —passages even supporting the short-life theory for which I am contending.

For instance, in Gen. xv. 15, the Lord said unto Abraham, "Thou shalt go to thy fathers in peace; thou shalt be buried in a *good old age*." Now, what did the Lord mean by "a good old age," and how did he fulfil this promise? Chapter xxv. 7, 8, will answer these questions. "And these are the days of the years of Abraham's life which he lived, an hundred and seventy and five years. Then Abraham gave up the ghost, and died in a good old age, an *old man*, and full of years; and was gathered unto his people."

Gen. xxxv. 28, 29. "And the days of Isaac were an hundred and eighty years; and Isaac gave up the ghost and died, and was gathered unto his people, being old and *full* of days."

How, I ask, could that promise have been given, or these two men be called "OLD and FULL of years," in the face of the fact that their term of life was far below that of their immediate ancestors, and not even a third of that which had been allotted to those more remote? Verily the writer must have penned these words with the knowledge, or the belief, that the ages of Abraham and Isaac surpassed those of their predecessors; otherwise, I cannot conceive what sense can be made out of such language as the above.

Again: Gen. xvii. 17. "Then Abraham fell upon his face and laughed, and said in his heart, Shall a child be born unto him that is an hundred years old, and shall Sarah that is ninety years old bear?" Also, xviii. 12. "Therefore Sarah laughed within herself, saying, After I am waxed old shall I have pleasure, my lord being old also?" This laugh of unbelief on their part bears its testimony in the same direction. What was the ground of it? It seemed to them contrary to the course of nature, inconsistent with their own observation and knowledge of human history. Had they understood these records of Genesis as they have been understood in modern times, and known that many of their ancestors had sons when largely over a hundred years of age, and lived almost to a thousand, they would not have regarded the announcement that they should have a son as at all strange, or laughed at the thought of it. There is much food for reflection in that laugh of old Abraham and Sarah.

Let us now take the testimony of Moses on the subject. He says in his prayer placed under the 90th Psalm: "Lord, Thou hast been our dwelling place in all generations. Before the mountains were brought forth, or ever Thou hadst formed the earth and the world, even from everlasting to everlasting Thou art God. Thou turnest man to destruction; and sayest, Return (to dust) ye children of men. . . All our days are passed away in Thy wrath. We spend our years as a tale that is told. The days of our years are three score years and ten; and if by reason of strength they be four score, yet is their strength labor and sorrow; for it is soon cut off, and we fly away.

Thus he asserts in the plainest terms that seventy and eighty years had been the ordinary limit of human life in all the previous ages of the world. And such it has been from his day to the present. Of all men, Moses is certainly a competent witness, being not only familiar with the history and language of his own people from the beginning, but also with all the ancient lore of Egypt. He was himself most probably over eighty years of age when he composed this Psalm. Though knowing that some of his ancestors had lived beyond a hundred years, he might still use such language with propriety; but not if their ages had, without exception, ranged from 133 all the way up to 969.

Lastly, Let us hear the words of Job (xiv. 1, 2, 5.) "Man that is born of a woman is of few days, and full of trouble. He cometh forth like a flower and is cut down. He fleeth also as a shadow, and continueth not. His days are determined, the number of his months are with Thee. Thou hast appointed his bounds that he cannot pass."

The author of Job must have been conversant with the Book of Genesis, for he says, "If I covered my transgression as Adam," in allusion to one of its statements.

Having shown what was the actual age of each patriarch from Adam to Noah, and the mean term of the whole to be 120 years, we shall continue the subject in the next chapter, and make it appear that it was of similar length from Noah to Abraham.

CHAPTER II.

THE LENGTH OF LIFE ACCORDING TO THE POSTDILUVIAN TABLE.*

THE ancient Hebrews seem to have possessed two distinct copies of Genesis, differing more or less from each other, like the Books of Kings and Chronicles, or the Four Gospels, but both held as sacred and authoritative. They are now known to us as the "Hebrew and Samaritan texts." Their apparent disagreement on points of chronology has sorely puzzled many eminent scholars, and various unsatisfactory explanations have been proposed. The view now advocated not only tends to harmonize the Bible chronology with reason and well known facts, but also the Hebrew and Samaritan texts with each other. This is done by supposing that the Hebrew text in the antediluvian table gives the years which the patriarchs lived *as men*, the Samaritan text the years they lived *as chiefs*. The order in the postdiluvian table is reversed, the Hebrew giving the

* Gen. xi. 10–37

years they lived as chiefs, the Samaritan the years they lived as men. It is highly probable that the verb "lived" would be employed there instead of "reigned," because it better expressed the nature of the patriarchal government. It is also, perhaps, the more ancient term.

As we are still only concerned with the length of their lives *as men*, we shall follow the Samaritan text in the postdiluvian catalogue, for the same reason that we followed the Hebrew in the antediluvian one. The age of Shem not being recorded, we only know he lived over 102 years, and we can do no better than give him an average number.

The account in the two texts stands thus:

			Sam. Text.				Heb. Text.	
Shem	lived	*as a man,*	137 (?) years.	*As a chief,*			—(?)yrs.	
Arphaxad	"	"	135	"	"		35	"
Salah	"	"	130	"	"		30	"
Heber	"	"	134	"	"		34	"
Peleg	"	"	130	"	"		30	"
Reu	"	"	132	"	"		32	"
Serug	"	"	130	"	"		30	"
Nahor	"	"	79	"	"		29	"
Terah	"	"	145	"	"	in Ur,	70	"

Making a mean of 128

That this is the true solution of the discrepancy

between the two texts may be seen, first, from the fact that the lives here in the Samaritan text most strikingly correspond in length with those of the Hebrew text in the antediluvian catalogue; second, from the fact that their lives, when thus reviewed, both before and after the flood, tally with those found between Abraham and Joshua, which are as follows:

Abraham lived as a man,	. .	175 years.
Sarah " "	. .	127 "
Ishmael " "	. .	127 "
Isaac " "	. .	180 "
Jacob " "	. .	147 "
Joseph " "	. .	110 "
Levi " "	. .	137 "
Kohath " "	. .	133 "
Amram " "	. .	137 "
Moses " "	. .	120 "
Aaron " "	. .	123 "
Joshua " "	. .	110 "

An average of 135 years for each of these. How striking the similarity all along the line?

From Adam to Noah, man's mean age is		120 years.
" Noah to Abraham, "	"	128 "
" Abraham to Joshua, "	"	135 "

Third, the Hebrew figures in the postdiluvian list are entirely too short for individual lives, and out of all proportion to those both before the flood and after the days of Abraham; but, on the other hand, they are in striking accord with the ordinary reigns of kings or chiefs—31 years. Fourth, the whole numbers attached to the names in both texts and in both tables are entirely too great for the lives of men, but agree most thoroughly with the duration of dynasties or governments, as I shall elsewhere make manifest.

Such, then, is the real teaching of our Scriptures as to the length of human life in the early ages of the world. Their statements, when thus understood, are at once freed from the charge of being mythical, and placed on a firm foundation, being sustained by the voice of history, both ancient and modern, as we will find by attending to what it says on the subject.

For instance: Manetho begins his thirty-one dynasties of Egypt with the reign of Menes, "the first of the mortal kings." The first dynasty, lying back in remote antiquity, had its seat in the city of This, and to it he assigns a period of 253 years duration, under eight successive sovereigns.

Now, if we allow the usual rate of one-third of their whole lives for *reign*, the account for the first five dynasties will stand thus:

	Length.	Kings.	Av. reign.	Whole life of each king.
I. Dynasty,	253 yrs.	8	31⅝ yrs.	95 yrs.
II. "	302 "	8	38 "	113 "
III. "	214 "	9	24 "	71 "
IV. "	284 "	8	35½ "	106 "
V. "	248 "	9	27½ "	82 "

Lenormant and Chevalier, in their excellent "Manual of Ancient History," regarding all of the "Thirty-one Dynasties of Manetho" as successive, put Menes (the head of the first) at 5004 B. C. Baron Bunsen, regarding them as mostly successive, puts him at 3643 B. C. Mr. Poole, regarding many of them as contemporary, reduces the time to 2717 B. C. Following Bunsen's date as the best—for recent researches tend to confirm it—then these five dynasties will cover that which is generally considered to be the antediluvian period of the world, and furnish ages, under the most liberal calculation, not surpassing 120 years. Even Mr. Poole's date sends Menes full 425 years beyond Usher's flood, and makes the five dynasties cover the times of Noah, Shem, Arphaxad, Salah, and Heber. Ages range from 71 to 113. Still further, Mr. Goodwin, a celebrated Egyptologist, has shown that 110 years was the utmost limit of ancient Egyptian life.

Again, the second Chaldean dynasty, according

to Berosus, lasted 234 years, under eight kings, which would give an average of only 88 years to each of them. It began, as estimated by Mr. George Rawlinson, 2286 B. C., and covers the interval between Salah and Terah, the father of Abraham. Its cotemporary Egyptian ones yield even a shorter term.

Yao Wong, the head of the first Chinese dynasty, which began 2205 B. C., lived, as stated in the books, 114 years; his successor, *Shun*, 110. This first dynasty itself lasted 439 years, under seventeen different emperors, with an average reign of 26, and whole life of about 77. The second dynasty lasted 644 years—twenty-eight emperors; average reign, 23; whole life, 69. These two dynasties extended from the days of Peleg to those of Solomon.

In the above calculations the short system, or Usher's Chronology, has been followed, of course, for the sake of argument.

Such, then, is the testimony of these venerable witnesses, corroborating my interpretation of the tables of Genesis as to the ages of the early patriarchs. These most ancient and reliable histories know nothing of human life reaching 200 years; neither do those of Assyria, Phœnecia, Greece, Rome, or modern times. Take the following from the New

American Cyclopædia, article Age, for its highest modern range. It says: "Pliny gives some instances of longevity taken exclusively from the region between the Apennines and the Po, as found in the census instituted by Vespasian; and within these narrow limits he enumerates fourteen persons who had attained the age of 110 years, twenty to the age of 125, forty the age of 130, forty the age of 135, thirty the age of 140, and one the age of 150.

Zeno is said to have lived 102, Democritus 104, Clovia 115, and numerous other similar cases are found recorded of ancient Greece and Rome, as well as of modern times and nations. Dr. Van Oven gives seventeen examples exceeding 150; and Mr. Bailey, in his Records of Longevity, a catalogue of over three thousand cases verging on to 100 or more, and not a few reaching as high as 150. Many of these may be more or less satisfactorily authenticated; and there can be no doubt of the comparatively frequent prolongation of human life to the age of 100, 110, 120, 130, 140; some even to 150, 160, 170; and in one known case to 185—a Hungarian peasant named Petrarch Czartan, who was born in A. D. 1587 and died in 1772.

Putting all these facts and arguments together,

we come to the conclusion that the Bible joins profane history in declaring that the *ordinary* limit of human life has always been from 70 to 80 years, the *ordinary extreme* limit from 130 to 150, and the *extraordinary* limit from 160 to 187. Of this last class only five individuals are mentioned in the Hebrew Scriptures—Jared, Methuselah and Lamech, before the flood; Abraham and Isaac after it. Even these have been equalled in modern times, according to the authority above quoted.

The Hebrews are a strong, well-built, sober, and peace-loving race. From the beginning they resided in a most genial and healthy climate, under a high moral and religious culture. These things, taken together, are sufficient to account for the fact that so great a number of their illustrious chiefs attained an age somewhat beyond the average limit.

The vital force, as well known, is greater in some cases than in others, and it is possible for us to believe that a few favored individuals may have lived the whole of 200 years; but when asked to believe that the patriarchs, or any other men, ever rose to the astounding age of 900 and more, we beg to decline till better proofs are presented than an unnatural interpretation of a few terse passages in the tables of Genesis.

If the reasons already brought forward be sufficiently strong to establish the fact that the patriarchs died as men at the end of the first dates attached to their names instead of begetting sons, then the remaining portions of the paragraph under review must also be understood in some way differing from the ordinary one; for Adam could not die, first at 130 years of age, and then again at 930, and be the same person; neither could any of the others mentioned in the lists.

Having ascertained the real import of the first sentence in our paragraph—that is, "Adam lived 130 years,"—we shall in the next chapter take up the second and third ones in order.

CHAPTER III.

ADAM, AT HIS DEATH, APPOINTED SETH HIS SPIRITUAL SUCCESSOR AND REPRESENTATIVE.

I. "AND he begat *a son* in his *own* likeness, after his image: And he called his name Seth." Notice, in the first place, that I have supplied the nominative *he*. This is correctly done; for the sentence is wholly independent, as to time, of its preceding one—"And Adam lived an hundred and thirty years." That such is the case is manifest from the fact that the verbs "lived," of the former, and "begat," of the latter, are non-correlative, or, in other words, they do not answer to each other.

Correlative verbs form dependent or connective sentences, as to time; non-correlative verbs, independent or disconnective ones. This is a *law* of all languages; and it may be illustrated by thousands of examples. Thus: Mr. Watson wrote a note and invited his friends to breakfast. He threw a stone and killed a bird. He lay down and slept. He lived sixty years and died. He died and was buried,

&c. These are correlative, and do not, according to our English idiom, require the repetition of the nominative.

Again: Mr. Watson graduated at Yale; and he took his seat in Congress when comparatively young. He lived to a good old age; and he begat seven sons. "Job lived, after this, 140 years; and he saw his sons, and his sons' sons, even four generations."* "And Adam lived 130 years, and he begat a son," &c. The verbs in all these being non-correlative, the sentences are disconnective as to time, and require the nominative to be repeated.

The verb *lived* so readily suggests its counterpart *died* that all speakers and writers are in the constant habit of leaving it to be supplied by the mind. Such, I maintain, is the case throughout the catalogues of Genesis. Notice, in the second place, that the words "a son" and "own" are not in the original text, but have been supplied by the translators. That the verb "begat" should occur here without its object being expressed is very remarkable, and very difficult to see the reason why. It is expressed in an exactly similar passage in the same chapter, (verse 28); "And Lamech lived 182 years: and he

* Dr. Conant's translation and punctuation.

begat a son (*ben*): And he called his name Noah." It is omitted only in two or three other places where the phraseology is much involved, but here it is quite simple.

"Beget" is one of those verbs which seems naturally to demand an object after it. Simply to say he begat, without saying son, daughter, child, heir, successor, or something of the kind, is certainly a very violent ellipsis, and hard to fill with absolute certainty. However, I will accept "a son" as the supply here, and pass on; but I reject "own" both as an unnecessary and an injurious addition. It makes the terms, "likeness and image," refer directly to the personal appearance and moral character of Adam, which, in all probability, is very far from what was intended by the author of the original text. As they occur in a table of dates and successions, is it not much more reasonable to suppose they refer to the fact that this son became Adam's heir or successor and representative in the patriarchal office, than to the irrelevant ones of physical form and moral traits? Not only so, but of what use would such a statement be? The author has no where told us whether Adam was well or ill favoured, white or brown, robust or slender, or anything whatever as to his moral peculiarities. The object with which another is compared must be previously known or described; for otherwise no sort of idea will be conveyed to the mind. "Likeness and image" are synonymous terms in English; were they necessarily such in the most ancient Hebrew? Or would any writer be likely to employ two words of exactly the same import, in such a very brief record as this, to express nothing? They seem to be here used in a sense of exaltation, as when first met with—Gen. i. 26: "And God said, Let us make man in our image after our likeness, and let them have *dominion* over the fish of the sea, and over the fowl of the air, and over the cattle, and over all the earth." By these words, then, man was made the heir of God, and given dominion over His earthly possessions. In similar language Christ is "appointed heir of all things." (Heb. i. 1 to 4.)

In this sort of sense I conceive Seth was said to be Adam's likeness and image, or successor and representative; but not in personal appearance or moral character. Was Seth more like his father in these repects than his brothers? If so, then this chosen son was morally the worst of the family, and these terms are used of him in a depreciatory way!

See 1 Cor. xv. 45 to 50. I cannot accept this view of the question.

Notice, in the third place, that our verb "begat" is much less comprehensive than its original *yolad*, which, among other things, means to make, to create, and to constitute. Besides, *yolad* in this sentence, and everywhere else in both tables, is in the *Hiphil*, or "Causative form" of the verb, a form that makes or causes its object to be, do, or become something different from that of the root, as will be shown elsewhere.

Now, we know that Seth was the *substitute* of Abel, who, by the favor of God, was constituted heir of the promises by faith. So Seth, by taking Abel's place, became the progenitor of the chosen race and Adam's successor as to things of a prophetic and religious nature. The sense of the two sentences, as I suppose, may be expressed about thus: "And he begat a son, whom he made his successor and representative; and he called his name, The Appointed One."

However, nothing of all which has been said under this head is really essential to my position, except that the sentence itself is independent of the preceding one, and affords no clue whatever to the time of Seth's birth. The next in order reads thus:

II. "And he called his name Seth," The Appointed One. The leading idea of the sentence, it seems to me, is that this younger son of Adam did not have the birthright *by nature*, but was *made* the heir of the religious promises *by appointment*, the name Seth being given him as significant of the fact.

But when did this important transaction take place—at Seth's birth or at Adam's death? I answer, at or near Adam's death; for this view alone is in keeping with the record, and the circumstances of the case. His mother had given him the name at his birth, but she then said nothing about his being the "likeness or image" of his father. But now Adam, the father, priest, and head of the house, gave or confirmed it to him after he had himself lived 130 years (a suitable time to die), an age above the average allotted to man, as I have heretofore conclusively shown. Again, this transaction stands as the last recorded act in Adam's history, and the name of Seth comes immediately after his in a long list of successions, that continue in an unbroken line down to Christ, the Head, Heir, and Antetype of all the promises.

How insignificant is the opinion that Adam, the progenitor and lord of the world, gave simply a name to a new-born infant, which was in personal appearance (for then it could have had no moral character) "the likeness and image of its father!"

How much more natural and reasonable, considering the place where it stands recorded, the dates and grand series of events that followed in Seth's line, to suppose that his father gave him the name or title, with all its implied rights, honors, and promises, in a solemn manner, while under the power of prophetic inspiration, near the close of his life.

Perhaps, also, from this early incident began the custom of "blessing," which continued down through the patriarchal ages even to the days of David. Look at Noah, as the last mentioned act of his life, pronouncing the blessing upon his three sons, and foretelling their future destiny; at Abraham, sending away the sons of his concubines to the east country, and giving all that he had to Isaac, the chosen heir with himself of the promises; at blind old Isaac, setting Jacob the younger before Esau the elder, and constituting him lord over his brethren; at Jacob, assembling his twelve sons around his dying couch, and announcing what should befall each of them in the last days. See him reject Reuben, his first-born, from "the excellency of dignity and the excellency of power," and bestow it upon his fourth son in these memorable words: "Judah, thou art he whom thy brethren shall praise; thy father's children shall bow down before thee; the sceptre shall not depart from Judah, nor a law-giver from between his feet, till Shiloh come." See him, as he makes an end of commanding them as to the rank and position of each one in the future kingdom of Canaan, gather up his feet in the bed, and yield up the ghost. Consider well this solemn scene, and you will get something like an adequate idea of what Adam did when he made his younger son his "likeness and image, and called his name Seth," or the Appointed One—appointed apparently in contradistinction to some other son who was by birth the actual head of the community, and with sole reference to the future. The "sceptre," given to Judah by Jacob at his death, only came into his hands in the person of his descendant, David, 640 years after the prophetic announcement.

Lastly, I would here ask, at what time do kings,

princes and priests appoint their successors in office—at the birth of their sons, or at the end of their own days? To ask the question is to answer it.

Having thus suggested the legitimate meaning of the first half of the paragraph, it will be necessary, before proceeding to the next half, to consider for a while the probable conditions of the Adamic family and government during its long existence of 930 years; for, as we have said before, if the founder of it lived only 130 years, then we are compelled to adopt a new interpretation of all that follows throughout the tables.

CHAPTER IV.

THE ADAMIC FAMILY AND GOVERNMENT RECONSTRUCTED.

1. WE should see in the term Adam, not only the name of the first man, but also that of the first family or historic government established among men. Under this name it began and continued to develop its own social, political and religious peculiarities during the long period of 930 years—time more than sufficient for the rise and fall of a mighty empire.

Let us reflect for a few moments in order to enlarge our ideas as to the probable population at its close. But we must here reason, as in mathematics, from the known to the unknown. For instance, the population of the United States has, since 1780, regularly doubled itself every twenty-three years—allowing for immigration, in about every twenty-six. Now, adopting the liberal number $33\frac{1}{3}$ as the standard of computation, and counting from the 130th year of Adam's life—supposing his family then composed of seventy persons, as in the case of Jacob—we shall have at the end of this first period one of the greatest nations that ever existed. Not only so, but such could be the case after leaving out the descendants of Cain to form another and independent community half as large. Thus reckoned, the population of Eden would have been at the end of the first 130 years, 70; at the end of the next 100 years, 560; at the end of the third, 4,480; at the end of the fourth, 35,840; at the end of the fifth, 286,720; at the end of the sixth, 2,293,760; at the end of the seventh, 18,350,080; at the end of the eighth, 146,800,640; at the end of the ninth, 1,174,405,120.

The actual result doubtless fell far below the vast sum obtained by the above mode of calculation, but then every thing favors the opinion that the primitive ages of the world were civilized, peaceful and highly conducive to the increase of population. The United States can scarcely be regarded as superior in this respect to Eden, Mesopotamia, China, and other favored portions of the globe. At all events we have the right to conclude that Adam became the historical name of a great nation, and after him Seth, Enos, &c.

II. If we would regard the "land of Eden" as the primitive Canaan or promised land, where the

Divine culture was begun and maintained during the first epoch of the world's history; the "garden" on the east of it as the original sanctuary; the Cherubim as stone images with sword in hand symbolically guarding the way to the Tree of Life, or the Most Holy Place in the "midst" of the garden; the original altar of sacrifice, as placed in front of the Cherubim, whither the people assembled themselves every Sabbath day to worship the Lord; and suppose that around these gradually arose the national temple and capital city of the empire, then we should come much nearer to the truth, I suspect, than our ordinary contracted notions of a pleasure garden bring us.

When reading the record of Adam and his times we should not allow a single pair of individuals to fill the mind or fix the attention too long; but we should pass rapidly on, associating with his, and every other name in the list, a nation, dynasty, or government of unusually long duration.

We should consider them as possessing at least the germs of the laws, customs, institutions, religious faith, doctrines and rites afterwards developed in the tabernacle, in the code of Moses, in the temple of

Solomon, in the synagogue, and finally in the Christian Church.

We should lay aside the conception of small tribes of rude, ignorant savages; for there is abundant proof in the Bible itself to show that man from the beginning was placed under the most intensely exacting moral and religious discipline—the very process by which barbarism is prevented, mental faculties developed, population increased, and a high state of civilization attained. The very dates or figures in the tables afford abundant evidence of great advancement; for savage tribes could never have kept such a record. Many of them are unable to count beyond twenty, and they all lose their history after a few centuries. But I do not propose to discuss this question, as it is not the one under consideration.

III. There is a good deal of reason for believing that Adam was the father of twelve sons, who became twelve tribes in the land of Eden; that it was apportioned to them for a special inheritance and dwelling-place, where they formed a confederacy similar to the one which the children of Israel afterwards formed in the land of Canaan.

In proof of this, let us hear Moses. He said to

his people in the thirty-second chapter of Deuteronomy: "Remember the days of old; consider the years of many generations; ask thy father and he will show thee; thy elders and they will tell thee; when the Most High divided to the nations (or tribes) their inheritance, when he separated the sons of Adam, he set the bounds of the people (in Eden) according to the number of the children of Israel."

Eden, then, was the original "holy land," the land where the first theocratic confederacy was established, and where the Divine cultus was embodied and perpetuated during the primitive ages of the world. It is the history of this government alone, in its various vicissitudes and changes of dynasty which is recorded in the first portions of Genesis. After the flood it seems to have been transferred to the land of Shinar, having the city of Ur for its principal seat until the days of Abraham, when it was removed to Canaan, Jerusalem becoming its distinguished metropolis down to the dispersion of the Jews.

From the twelve sons of Adam and their tribal divisions in the original land of Eden, we may account for the fact that the number twelve, at a very early day, became a sacred number among the

Hebrews and various other western Asiatic nations. In the Bible alone we have the twelve tribes of Canaan (including the Perizzites), the twelve tribes of Joktan, of Nahor, of Ishmael, of Israel, and finally the twelve Apostles of Christ, the founders of the Church—the last phase of the kingdom of God on earth.

Says the learned Kitto: "The Persians, as well as other oriental peoples, still have geographical and ethnological divisions according to the number twelve," and he infers from many reasons, "that it was held in so much favor among them that, when possible, doubtful cases were adapted to it."

Further, Jewish tradition has always assigned to Adam more sons than the three mentioned by name. We know that Cain was the eldest, and had the right by the law of nature or primogeniture to succeed his father in the government of the community. But we learn that "God had respect unto Abel;" that is, chose him to be heir of the promises by faith, and Adam's successor as to things pertaining to the kingdom to come.

This prophetic election of Abel did not of itself affect the natural rights of Cain, but he so understood it, and in the anger of his jealousy, rose up and slew his brother. That he slew him in order to preserve his birthright to the headship of the family after the death of his father, is evident from these words: "And the Lord said unto Cain, Why art thou wroth ? And why is thy countenance fallen ? If thou doest well shalt thou not have the *excellency ?* (and if thou doest not well, sin lieth at the door) and unto thee shall be his desire (Abel's submission), and thou shalt *rule over him*." (Gen. iv. 6, 7.)

The same kind of difficulty arose in the family of Isaac: "And Esau hated Jacob because of the blessing wherewith his father blessed him; and Esau said in his heart, the days of mourning for my father are at hand; then will I slay my brother Jacob. He took away my birthright; and, behold, now he hath taken away my blessing." (Gen. xxvii.)

Cain, for this act of murder, was banished from the land of Eden, and, like Esau, went beyond its sacred borders to the land of Nod, where he and his posterity established the second great historical kingdom of the world, with the walled city of Enoch for its capital. Its history is given for a few generations in the fourth chapter of Genesis, and then dropped, as is the case throughout the Bible with all those branches which did not belong to the chosen line.

Judging from the fact that Cain and Abel were both engaged in their respective occupations of farming and sheep-raising before bringing their "offerings unto the Lord"—done apparently as their own voluntary acts—we infer that they were then mature men, perhaps as much as forty years of age. Then, on the death of Abel, Adam's family, according to the course of human events, would have been about complete, and his third son a full grown man. On the banishment of Cain from the land of Eden, this third son would naturally have succeeded to the forfeited birthright, and at his father's death become the head of the house of Adam. The secular government of Eden would descend in the line of his eldest son from one generation to another; till, from corruption or some other cause, the regular succession was broken up.

These chiefs, all reigning under one common name or title, constituted the first period of 930 years, the house or dynasty of Adam; which, in brief tabular language, is simply called Adam, as in China, where the various dynasties or reigning families are simply called Hia, Shang, Chen, Tsin,

Han, &c., without any kind of qualifying epithet. As the mode of using proper names will be discussed in another chapter, let us further continue to examine into the probable conditions of the Adamic family and government.

Allowing forty years of rule to each of Adam's successors, then the house bearing his name consisted of twenty-one chiefs, including himself. Seth would not be among the number, for we know that he was born after the death of Abel, and was, therefore, not the third, but most probably the youngest son of the family. We may suppose him, like Isaac, born out of due season, since his mother's remarks at his birth show plainly that she regarded him as the special "gift of God," the child of promise "instead of Abel whom Cain slew." He was, then, by *substitution* made the progenitor of the elect branch of the house, and the heir of the kingdom by faith—a kingdom to come. Accordingly, he did not himself enter upon its actual possession, but like Abraham, Isaac, Jacob, Judah, and the other Old Testament worthies, waited in hope for the promised inheritance. Thus eight hundred long years passed away, and generation after generation of his sons died in faith without receiving even the first instalment of the promises. (See Heb. xi., &c.)

The tribe of Seth during this waiting time were subject to the government of Adam's third son and his successors in office. As it was the elect and most virtuous member of the confederacy, it would multiply more rapidly in wisdom and numbers, while the ruling one would tend to corruption and decay. On the fall of the house of Adam, the prince of the house of Seth, or some other chosen member of the tribe, ascended the throne of Eden, and with him the tribe itself became the ruling people of the land. And thus the original Seth, like Abraham, obtained in his descendants the promised inheritance.

The government of Eden remained with this *latter Seth* and the family of his *eldest son* for 912 years, constituting the second period, or dynasty of Seth. Enos, being the *younger* and chosen son of this latter Seth the founder of the dynasty, was the heir expectant during its existence. On the fall of the house of Seth, the prince of the house of Enos took possession of the government, which, in its turn, continued with his eldest son's posterity for 905 years, constituting the third period, or dynasty of

Enos, Cainan being heir elect during its reign. The succession was thus transmitted from period to period, the secular government following the law of nature or primogeniture, the religious promises the law of election and faith.

In the Scriptures, the eldest is never the "chosen son." From Abel to David he is, when mentioned, invariably a younger son of the patriarch, and waits in faith and hope for the promised blessing. On the other hand, the eldest son is always the one "born after the flesh," and finally cast out. Such, in short, is the Divine method of teaching the great doctrine that the "gifts and callings of God are not of works, but of grace, not to those born after the flesh, but to those born after the Spirit."

Before leaving this section, let me remind the reader that the above supposed mode of transmitting the secular government, together with the religious promises, from one period or chief patriarch to another, claims for itself only a certain kind of probability and consistency with the general teachings of the Scriptures. It is only designed to show that, after the received interpretation of the tables shall have been overthrown, there remains this, or *some other allowable way* of understanding them;

and that we are under no necessity whatever either to reject their historic value, or to accept a mass of absurdities.

II. Neither the Jews nor any other nation ever did, or ever could reckon time by the ages of fathers at the birth of sons. Such a thing has always been a moral impossibility. Genealogy is far too complicated a matter for such a purpose. In a few generations it would become hopelessly involved. Dates are attached to the reigns of kings, to the rise of dynasties, or to prominent events of some kind, not to the birth of children. Births are private affairs, and in no way attract the attention of a community, or affect its social and political status. Besides, births and deaths in royal households, especially among polygamists, are constantly occurring —so constantly as to render it impossible for the reigning sovereign to determine much before his own death which son should ascend the throne, even if he wished to do so. Supposing he did so, how then could he announce the fact to all his subjects, and require them to keep their dates accordingly? Such a mode of procedure would certainly presuppose a magnificent system of post offices, if not of telegraphic wires! Would any king like to have his subjects keeping their dates in the name of his son rather than in his own?

Again, if the death of the heir appointed should often happen, or the father often change his mind as to his successor, would not his people soon become disgusted with such an ever fluctuating standard of time, and adopt some more permanent one for their own convenience?

Men of our days are unable to remember the ages of their grandfathers at the birth of their own fathers; why, then, should we regard the memories of the ancients as so much better than that of the moderns, or attribute to them such mental feats, even impossibilities? Why consider them so unlike known humanity, and perpetually subject to a course of most stupendous and contradictory miracles? True, miracles have their place in the economy of Divine revelation, but have we the right to manufacture them in order to get over difficulties? Mankind in all ages have followed the same mental laws, been under the same necessity of dividing time into periods, and preserving the relation of current events by comparing them with some other more prominent ones.

Dates become fixed by a community or nation constantly using them in their conversation and business transactions, and so the most important ones are transferred to written history and handed down to future generations.

The Chinese are the most remarkable people in the world for preserving ancient customs and forms of speech, as well as family registers. Many of these registers go back for hundreds, some even for thousands of years; but they never note the ages of fathers at the birth of sons—only the birth and death of individuals according to the date of the Emperor's reign. In common conversation they frequently speak of so many "generations of men or generations of dynasties," but they never date their documents or their histories according to generations of any kind. They invariably keep time by reigns, dynasties, and cycles. Such, from its naturalness, would seem to have been the case among all civilized nations since the beginning of man upon the earth. The Jews, whose ancestors preserved the chronological tables in the book of Genesis, did not constitute an exception in any sense to this rule; for they also reckoned by the reigns of their judges and kings in ordinary matters; in those of a general nature, by important events in their history, as the call of

Abraham, the exodus, the building of the temple, the captivity, &c. Every one knows that their chronology does not run according to the birth of sons. To their many genealogical registers, both in the Old and New Testaments, no dates or figures of any sort are attached. They simply say such an one begat such an one, or was the son of such an one. In all the Bible the ages of but three men at the birth of their sons are specified, to wit: Shem, Abraham, and Isaac—and this apparently, not for chronological purposes, but to show the power of God, as they were unusually old at the time.

From these various considerations, may we not lawfully conclude that the figures in the registers from Abraham to Adam are also not birth dates, but death dates, first of the chief patriarchs themselves, and then of the governments going under their respective names?

In these ancient bits of history, we have genealogy, chronology, and election, all combined in language most remarkable for brevity and comprehensiveness —giving in less than two short chapters the rise and fall of nineteen successive houses, surpassing in duration the most favored ones known to have ever existed. All are the lineal descendants of one chosen progenitor, and one after the other, founded by a chosen head. How meagre, unsatisfactory, and full of difficulties is the common understanding that makes them a mere succession of individual men, unconnected with any kind of government, national life, or public incident whatever! History with history left out! Men noted only for three things: 1st, For living a marvelously long life; 2nd, For begetting a certain son when disproportionately young; 3rd, For then waiting over seven hundred years and begetting other "sons and daughters" in the year of their death! We shall in another place expose these inconsistencies; for it is a sad fact that men will, without examination, adopt the most absurd opinions, or reject the most certain truths.

We must now return and take up the remaining portion of the paragraph with which we set out. But before doing so, allow me to suggest that the facts and arguments already offered are entitled to their full weight in determining its meaning; for it is not allowable to suppose that the two parts are inconsistent with each other. The same person could not die at 130 years of age, then live 800 more and beget sons and daughters, or die again at 930.

5

CHAPTER V.

THE LATTER HALF OF THE PARAGRAPH.—THE HOUSE OF ADAM CONTINUED EIGHT HUNDRED YEARS AFTER ADAM'S DEATH.

THE first two sentences in the latter half of the paragraph, which is now to come up for discussion, read thus in our English translation: "And the days of Adam after he begat Seth were eight hundred years; and *he* begat sons and daughters."

Notice that in this place only the nominative "he" has been inserted before this oft-repeated statement. It is correctly supplied here, and should have appeared in all the others. The ambiguity which has produced most of the difficulty, and led scholars astray in their chronological reckonings, lies in the first member of this verse. It has caused them, on the one hand, to make the life of individual men far too long; and on the other, the life of the race far too short. The ambiguity is found in the Hebrew manner of using the proper names Adam, Seth, Enos, &c., and also in the verb *yolad*, here rendered invariably by the verb "begat." To make this appear will be the burden of the first two sections of this chapter, taking up first the names, then the verb.

I. Proper names, with us, are now divided into several classes, among which are Personal, Family, National, and Ethnographical; but the book of Genesis knows nothing of such divisions. It was written before the origin of these distinctions, and in it one name only fills the office of these four. This fact must be kept constantly in mind, otherwise we may make the most serious mistakes, by putting our own modern ideas on to the ancient text.

All are familiar with the fact that the Old Testament calls families, tribes and nations after the names of their founders; that each of those mentioned in the tenth chapter of Genesis is the name both of a man and of a nation. This is apparent, not only from the fact that many of them have a plural termination, but also from the closing words of every paragraph, and of the chapter itself. Thus:

"By these (sons and grand sons of Japheth named above) were the isles of the Gentiles divided in their lands; every one after his tongue, after their families, in their nations."

"These are the sons of Ham after their families, after their tongues, in their countries, and in their nations."

"These are the sons of Shem, in their families, after their tongues, in their lands, after their nations."

"These are the families of the sons of Noah, after their generations, in their nations: and by these were the nations divided in the earth after the flood."

The tenth chapter of Genesis is the great ethnological chart of the world; hence Josephus is very particular to tell us how all the postdiluvian nations bore the names of their progenitors, the immediate descendants of Noah, and also how some of them, through the influence of time, had lost their original designations. The Hebrews, we know, called the Medes, Madai; the Greeks, Javan, from sons of Japheth; the Ethiopians, Cush; the Egyptians, Mestre; the Phoenecians, Canaanites, from sons of Ham; others, Elam, Asshur, Aram, &c., from sons of Shem. In fact, those personal names got a place in that short chapter because they had become national, and therefore of historical importance. Otherwise we should never have heard of them. The same peculiarity is continued through the more modern books of the Bible, Edom, Ammon, Moab,

Midian, Israel, Judah, and scores of others, being indiscriminately the names of a man and also of a nation.

Now, if the names mentioned immediately after the flood, as well as those more remote from it, all have this double sense and application, why should not the same be true of those mentioned before it? In the very nature of things it must be so. The book, the language, and the people who preserved them, all exhibit, from first to last, a striking consistency, and therefore Adam, Seth, Enos, Cainan, and the other antediluvian names in the catalogue severally indicate either the progenitor himself, the family, nation or government which sprang from him, as the context and subject matter of the record may require. Had not those persons become something more than mere individuals their names would not have been honored with those accompanying figures and dates, or remained to this late day.

Did ever private persons leave behind them such a register with so many dates attached? Never, and never will; for it is a moral impossibility. Figures despise a plebeian name, but rush to score the years of royal fame. How very far from the truth of the case is the common conception that these patriarchal titles correspond to our given names Peter, James, John, and Charles; yet this lies at the foundation of the received interpretation! If there were any such names in those early days they have not come down to us.

Again, it is the constant habit of the Old Testament to use its personal names first in a specific, then in a generic sense, without the least reserve or notification of the change. This is done sometimes in alternate verses, sometimes in the same verse. Hundreds of examples in illustration of the fact may be readily produced; but a few specimen passages must suffice. For instance, it is said in Genesis xlvii. 27: "And Israel dwelt in the land of Goshen"— meaning both Jacob and his whole family.

Genesis xlvii. 29: "And the time drew near that Israel must die"—meaning only Jacob.

Genesis xlix. 24: "From thence is the Shepherd, the Stone of Israel"—meaning the nation.

Judges vi. 6: "And *Israel* was greatly impoverished because of the Midianites; and the *children* of Israel cried unto the Lord." Here the name Israel means first the nation, second the father of the nation.

Judges x. 9, 10: "Moreover, the children of Ammon passed over Jordan, to fight against Judah and against Benjamin, and against the house of Ephraim; so that Israel was sore distressed; and the children of Israel cried unto the Lord." Observe how the word "house" is left off before Judah and Benjamin, and written before Ephraim; also how it is first "Israel" then "the children of Israel." In both forms of expression the sense is the same.

Exodus ii. 1: "And there went a man of the house of Levi, and took to wife a daughter of Levi." Now, had the word "house" been omitted before Levi, in the first case as in the second, it would have made no difference in the meaning; for "Levi" and "the house of Levi," "Israel" and "the house of Israel," "the children of Israel," "the kingdom of Israel," "Judah," "the house of Judah," or "kingdom of Judah," and the like, are used one for the other indiscriminately. Finally the name Adam itself is also used in this interchangeable manner, as in—

Genesis iv. 25: "And Adam knew his wife again, and she bare a son." Here it is specific, personal, and masculine gender.

Chap. v. 2: "Male and female created he them, and called their name Adam." Here it is the generic name of mankind, and both masculine and feminine.

Chap. v. 3: "And Adam lived an hundred and thirty years." Here it is again specific and personal.

Chap. v. 4: "And the days of Adam after he begat Seth were eight hundred years" Here it is again generic, being equivalent to the "house" of Adam, as I conceive.

Chap. v. 5: "And all the days that Adam lived were nine hundred and thirty years." Here the two senses are united into one, becoming the name of both the founder and the house, or government. After these nine hundred and thirty years the nation ceased to be styled Adam. The dynasty being changed, it was next called Seth, then Enos, and so on down to Abraham, where *tabulated* history closes, and *detailed* history begins.

The reader must be content with this mere outline of what might be said on the Bible mode of using its proper names, and allow me to pass on to the verb "begat."

II. The Hebrew verb *yolad* is a generic or very comprehensive term, requiring several English ones to translate it through all its various changes of form and signification. On the other hand, *beget* is specific, having but one definite sense through every form, mood, and tense.

Gesenius gives, among the *active* meanings of *yolad*—"1st. To bear, or bring forth as a mother; also, to take effect. 2d. To beget as a father; to create, to produce, to constitute, to appoint. 3d. To declare one's pedigree, or to give one's name to be enrolled in the registers, as in Numbers i. 18; to cause to bring forth; to make fruitful."

Passive: "To be born, to be brought forth, to be created, as the mountains in Psalms xc. 2."

Parkhurst gives "become" as among its meanings, citing Job. xi. 12, in illustration—"Vain man would be wise; though a wild ass's colt, he would *become* a man!"

Gesenius quotes Job xxxviii. 8, 9, 28, 29, and Deut. xxxii. 18, to show that it has the sense of to create, to produce; and Psalms ii. 7, to show that it is used for constitute, or appoint—"I have set my king upon my holy hill of Zion. I will declare the decree: the Lord hath said unto me, Thou art my son, this day have I begotten thee (constituted thee as king)."

Observe here how the "decree" of the Lord made, created, or constituted his son king of Zion. The same idea is similarly expressed by St. Paul in the first chapter of Hebrews.

We thus see how much more varied are the shades of signification in *yolad* than in the English word begat, or any one similar verb in our language; and how it may require several of them for its translation. In fact *yolad* strikingly resembles the Greek *geno*, or the Latin *gigno* in its uses. These, it is well known, express not only parentage, but also the act of elevating persons to rank or office. Moreover, the New Testament writers, for the purpose of exalting persons, constantly employ the words beget, born, son, child, heir, and the like; and these writers were all Hebrews, and wrote with Hebrew conceptions in their minds. We create, make, or appoint earls, dukes, and bishops.

Let the reader also be careful to notice that *yolad* is repeated three times in every paragraph of both tables, and that they are all of the *hiphil* or *causative* form of the verbal root—the first and third ones being in the indicative mood, future tense; and the second in the infinitive. Each form of the Hebrew verb has its own appropriate name; as, kal, hiphil, hophul, &c., with its own peculiar shade of meaning.

Gesenius in his grammar says that, "From the stem are produced, according to an unvarying analogy in all verbs, the various derivative forms, each distinguished by a specific change in the stem, with a corresponding *definite change in its signification.*" He then gives several examples to show how the sense of the verb changes in passing from one of these forms to another; among which are the the following, under the head Hiphil: "Kal or stem, to *go* forth; Hiphil, to *lead* forth. Kal, to be holy; Hiphil, to *make holy*, or sanctify. Kal, to perish; Hiphil, to *destroy*. Kal, to be heavy; Hiphil, to *make heavy*. Kal, to be rich; Hiphil, to *become rich*." To these let me add a few taken at random from the Old Testament; as, David *came* to Hebron; they *brought* Joseph into Egypt. To trust; to *make one trust*. To eat; to *cause him to eat*. To remember; to *make mention of*. To live; to *save or restore life*.

Thus it is plain that the hiphil form of the verb *yolad*—the one used throughout the tables—*makes* or *causes* persons and things to do, or become something other than that expressed by the kal, its root. Hence, it appears that each of the patriarchs made or caused one of the sons whom he begat to become an heir, a prince, successor, representative, or something more than a mere son. This peculiarity of the hiphil form of the verb is well shown in Genesis xvii. 20: "As for Ishmael, I have heard thee: twelve *princes* shall he beget, and I will make *him* a great nation." That is, he should beget twelve *sons*, who should become twelve princes—sons are *born* or begotten, princes are *made* or become such. It is also worthy of note that the kal form, past tense, is employed for giving the pedigrees in the fourth and tenth chapters, rendered thus in our Bible: "And Irad begat Mehujael: and Mehujael begat Methusael: and Methusael begat Lamech." In tenth chapter: "And Cush begat Nimrod: and Mizraim begat Ludim: and Canaan begat Zidon: Arphaxad begat Salah; and Salah begat Heber."

How, then, is it, let me ask, that though in the tables of the fifth and eleventh chapters the form of the verb is changed from the kal past to the hiphil future, nothing is said by our translators indicating the accompanying change in its signification? They have rendered both forms by "begat," as if they were the very same in sense. Did the original writer make this marked difference without design or perception of any distinction in their import? It cannot be so; for what then would become of the law laid down so confidently by Gesenius in the words before quoted—"The various derivative forms of the verb are each distinguished by a specific change in the stem, with a corresponding definite change in its signification?" Why was not the English reader given the benefit of this "definite change of signification?" Doubtless because our word begat is wholly incapable of expressing the *causative idea* contained in the hiphil form of *yolad*. For it seems to have the double sense of both a *lineal* and *official* descent in all the registers of the chosen branch of Adam—a conception which no one word in our vocabulary can fully express.

Yet this is nothing unusual or strange; for there are words in every language which cannot be perfectly rendered into another. As our version of the Bible brings out only the *lineal* sense of the verb, I shall endeavor to bring out the *official*, and the reader, by putting the two together, will get its full import as used in the table. Thus: "And the days of Adam, after the appointment of his son Seth, were 800 years." By being particular to observe that the previous verse closed with the words, "He called his name the *Appointed One*," we will readily see how our sentence, by keeping up this leading idea of its antecedent, counts the 800 years, not from the time of Seth's birth (which is not specified), but from the time he was called or *made the Seth*. If this be so, then the 800 years indicate the period that elapsed between his elevation to the heirship of the promises and their realization, or the days of the house of Adam after the death of its founder.

By the aid of Hebrew concordances I have traced the verb *yolad* through the whole of the Old Testament, and carefully studied the reasons for its changes of form, especially from the kal to the hiphil; and I noted the following interesting facts:

1st, In the genealogies of ordinary persons, of sons of concubines and rejected branches, the kal, or some other mode of expression other than the hiphil of begat, is invariably employed.

2nd, The hiphil is used in all of the regular registers of the chosen line from Adam to David.

3rd, It is used of the princes of the leading families in the honored tribes of Judah, Joseph, and Benjamin, but never of the others.

4th, Also always of the High Priests, from Aaron till after the "restoration."

5th, The sudden, even abrupt, change of form

when one or the other of these classes comes in the lists, is frequently very marked, and indicative of evident design.

6th, The hiphil seems to be the form of *honor* or *elevation*, by which both the blood and dignities of patriarchs, prominent chiefs, kings, and high priests are transmitted.

7th, Outside of the registers it frequently, though not always, implies something of the same kind.

Our verb beget, being a sensuous one in its meaning, fails to express these shades of thought, and, consequently, they are entirely lost to the readers of the English version of the Scriptures. In our democratic language, patriarchs, kings, and priests are born, eat, drink, live, and die like common mortals; but such is not the case in most Asiatic nations. With them almost every act of their sovereigns and high functionaries must be set forth in other than ordinary vulgar terms—in what is called "the official style." This peculiar custom is also known to be very ancient.

Is it not then far more probable that the verb *yo-lad* should have this sort of compound and elevating sense in the pedigrees of those most noble and illustrious patriarchs, than that they should have lived as men to the great age of over 900 years? Considering all the serious difficulties which such longevity involves, is it not putting far too much strain on reason and faith? But I cannot discuss this point further, lest my work should swell beyond the bounds fixed for the whole question. I have said sufficient to suggest a train of thought and research for all who may be inclined to investigate it for themselves.

In conclusion, I feel fully justified in saying that this sentence puts us under no verbal or grammatical necessity to believe that Adam begat Seth when 130 years old, and then lived 800 more; but leaves us at full liberty to hold that, having appointed him his spiritual heir at the former date, he died; while the community bearing his name continued to exist as a government of some sort till the end of the latter, when it was succeeded, according to the record, by the house of Seth.

II. The next sentence in order is: "And he begat sons and daughters."

The "he" occurring here, as said before, though correctly supplied, is not in the original, and there is no more reason for inserting it in this than in the other parallel cases, which are all without it. Now, if any one is bold enough to contend that the first two sentences in the paragraph are connected in time, and Seth was, therefore, born at the end of the 130 years, then he is bound to hold that those additional "sons and daughters" were born at the end of the 800. And what monstrous absurdities it involves! Adam begat three sons in the first 130 years of his life, then after skipping 800 more, has an indefinite number of them in the year of his death!! But not only so; all the other patriarchs, one after the other, performed the same strange and wonderful feats!!! If to get out of this difficulty he should say they were born, not at the end, but during that term, then he admits the truth of my position, that the time of Seth's birth is not specified, and with the admission his short chronology goes by the board. "That which proves too much proves nothing," is an axiom in logic.

Some may ask who were these "sons and daughters?" I unhesitatingly answer, the kings and queens who, in succession, ruled over the house of Adam during the 800 years that followed his death. There is no mention whatever here made of the common people. This table was doubtless taken from the royal registers of the nation, like all other documents of the kind, and because of its chronological, religious and other uses, was very carefully preserved and handed down from age to age. Ordinary men leave no such records behind them, for the very good reason that, being of no public utility or concern, they soon disappear.

III. The last two sentences in the paragraph are: "And all the days that Adam lived were nine hundred and thirty years; and he died."

These are but the summing up of what had been stated above. No additional information whatever is given. Any one can add the two preceding numbers together and obtain the 930. This, in all probability, was done by some later hand, for the sake of convenience; but still at a very early date. No objection, however, can be offered to it on this account, for it is mathematically certain, and that kind of certainty is of the highest grade.

The postdiluvian table is left in its original condition, with the numbers unadded up, nothing being said about the death of the later patriarchs. The last sentence reads: "And he died." It is as proper to say this of a nation, dynasty, or government, according to the Bible style, as of an individual; for the pronoun "he" often stands either for the one or for the other; while "die" is also so employed, as may be illustrated by the following passages:

Numbers xxiv. 20: "And when Balaam looked on Amalek he took up his parable, and said, Amalek was the first of the nations; but his latter end shall be that *he perish* for ever."

Verse 24: "And ships shall come from the coast of Chittim, and shall afflict Asshur, and shall afflict Heber, and *he* also shall perish for ever."

Hosea xiii. 1: "When Ephraim spake trembling, he exalted himself in Israel; but when he offended in Baal, *he died.*" That is, the nation of Israel, now going under the name of Ephraim, died as a nation or government, though millions of the people continued to live. If we did not have the origin of the name Ephraim, with the modifications of meaning through which it afterwards passed, we should certainly understand this passage of the individual son of Joseph—and how wide it would be of the mark! But not wider than the one-man interpretation of the patriarchal names of which we have been treating.

We are now through with all the various statements in the first paragraph in the antediluvian table. It is not necessary to treat of those which follow it, as they are substantially the same; the import of the model being ascertained, we have it of all the others.

We may sum up the matter thus: First comes the name of the founder of each dynasty, with the length of his life; then the name of the son appointed as heir and successor to the promises by faith; then the number of years intervening between the giving and the fulfilment of the promise; then the whole period of the national existence under the denomination of Adam; and lastly, its termination, fall, or death as a government; then comes its successor, the house of Seth, which is in turn treated in the same manner.

I have thus endeavored briefly to show how the book of Genesis is to be understood as giving a list of houses or dynasties, following each other in chronological order, rather than a succession of individual men. Consequently the whole numbers under the several patriarchal names must be added together in order to ascertain the length of time between the days of Adam and the birth of Abraham—a term at least equal to 10,500 years.

What mighty issues hang on this question! Viewed in this manner, those venerable tables of

Genesis open up for us a highway through what is generally called the pre-historic ages of the world, and at once become the most important documents of the kind in the possession of man.

The remaining portion of this little work will be devoted to showing how its long chronology is sustained by reason, by other parts of the Bible, and by facts from various sources.

THE CORRECTNESS OF THE DYNASTIC THEORY OF INTERPRETATION, WHICH ASSIGNS A SHORT LIFE TO INDIVIDUALS AND A LONG LIFE TO THE RACE, IS ARGUED FROM ITS REASONABLENESS, GENERAL AGREEMENT WITH THE TEACHINGS OF THE BIBLE, HISTORY, SCIENCE, TRADITION, AND MYTHOLOGY.

CHAPTER VI.

THE DYNASTIC SCHEME OF CHRONOLOGY IN HARMONY WITH REASON.

1. IT is reasonable to suppose that the facts and events regarded by men of modern times as of first importance and worthy of public record, are the ones most likely to have been preserved from the beginning. Among these, as all experience shows, are the doings of kings, the length of reigns, the duration of dynasties, and the rise and fall of nations; but never the ages of fathers at the birth of sons.

2nd, It is the custom of historians to divide the national life of which they treat into periods according to the various dynasties or governments under which it had existed, and, at the end of their books, to add a brief summary or chronological table. In these they frequently only mention the general name or title of the royal family, with the years of its duration, the number of its sovereigns, &c. Such tables, from their great utility and convenience of form, are very tenacious of life; and such, it is natural to conclude, are those found preserved in the book of Genesis, and not a mere list of individual births and deaths.

3rd, Our theory assigns a reasonable age for the birth of children, the death of men, and the fall of ruling houses in ancient times; while the common one is far otherwise. According to the latter, the the antediluvian patriarchs, leaving out Noah, lived on an average 803 years, and had their sons as early as 117—the one mentioned by name being most probably not the oldest; whereas, if there be any truth in the opinion that those who live long mature slowly, they should have had them from 275 to 300; or men now should become fathers at six to ten years of age!

Then, all of a sudden, the case is reversed, and Noah is regarded as disproportionately old, and made to beget his three sons, Shem, Ham, and Japheth in his 500th year! But this is not all. In the third chapter of Luke there are fifty-five generations of men from Christ to Abraham—say in a space of 2,000 years.

Fortunately, we have ample information as to what was the common limit of life in that period, and know it was about seventy. By calculation we find that sons were born to them at an average of 36½ years of age; but from Abraham to Noah, when life, as currently held, reached the high mean of 313 years, it was only 31½, and beyond the flood, still more out of proportion—a perfect inversion of the whole course and order of nature, without any apparent cause or assignable reason!! The dynastic mode of interpretation, on the other hand, performs no such feats, encounters no such difficulties, carries no such weight, but glides smoothly through the whole stream of time.

4th, Still further, the common theory, when worked out, presents other most remarkable facts and figures. Thus, if the sons of the antediluvian patriarchs succeeded their fathers in the government, as stated by Josephus, and held by commentators, then they would have had to wait, on an average, 803 years, in order to reign comparatively very few— similar to kings of our day ascending their thrones one after another at about sixty-four, and dying of old age at seventy. Even on their accession they would have been too old, feeble, and inefficient generally for the discharge of the public duties. Surely no people ever did submit to such an arrangement. In more recent times, kings have reigned about one-third of their whole lives; but these only an eighth of theirs, while two of them never reached the throne at all! The account stands as follows: Adam reigned 930 years, Seth 112, Enos 98, Cainan 95, Mahalaleel 55, Jared 132, Enoch fell short of the throne, having gone to heaven in his youth, 435 years before the death of his father; then Methuselah reigned 669, and Lamech died five years before his father! Does not this kind of succession seem rather strange and freaky? But, as such things were the order of the day in those ancient times, it doubtless seemed all natural enough to them!

5*th*, Again, men who were the contemporaries of Adam himself for more than 175 years were drowned in the flood, and mankind, except eight persons, were destroyed in less than two lifetimes from their origin! How God seems in haste, contrary to His revealed character of long-suffering and patience, to exterminate a race whom He had just created, and to whom, as individuals, He had granted the most remarkable longevity! He cannot even wait till His word of promise is fulfilled, but cuts them off twenty years before the term allotted for their repentance had expired!! How could man become so utterly corrupt, "every imagination of the thoughts of his heart only evil continually, the earth filled with violence," and the patience of a merciful God exhausted in so short a time as 1,656 years? Such has not been the ordinary course of providence. On the contrary, the dynastic scheme of chronology furnishes 7,737 years for their growth and consummation, and brings all into harmony with the ways of man and God.

6*th*, Could men, especially patriarchs, kings, and chiefs, pass through such a state of corruption and violence as this, one after another for ten generations, and reach the high average of more than 800 years without getting killed in some way? Then, if those days were as full of wars, murders, accidents, and nameless dangers as ours, they must have been, like Achilles, invulnerable. If our constitutions had sufficient vital force within them to send us up to that great age, the most of us would fall by some kind of violence or accident long before reaching it.

It is indeed doubtful whether the rulers of any nation have ever escaped for half that period. The English sovereigns, beginning at A. D. 946, have been killed at the intervals of 33, 37, 50, 21, 13, 99, 128, 158, 166 years—the last 228 having now passed without a violent death. In Germany, the intervals, as far as examined, have been 36, 19, 188, 120. In France, rather better, about 500 years once coming together without such an incident; but as I have mislaid the statistics I cannot give the details. In China, reckoning from A. D. 589 to the present time, the matter stands thus: Two emperors were slain in 31 years, five in 287, two in 16, one in 13, one in 11, one in 2, four in 176, three in 88, three in 276, and none in the last 232. The rate in the kingdoms of Israel and Judah is about the same as those above given; while, as every one knows, in Greece, Rome, and Persia, natural death was the exception rather than the rule.

7th, Were all the laws of nature reversed somewhere between the present and the patriarchal ages; and if so, where is the proof? Are we at liberty to interpret the Bible, or any other historical document, so as to confuse the whole order of things? Are we not wrong when one difficulty after another can be piled upon us like "Ossa on Pelion?" Can we rest comfortably under such a pressure? A horse whose bones are all out of joint is useless as a horse; and such is the condition of the usual interpretations of the catalogues of Genesis, together with all the systems of chronology based upon them. They should be abandoned at once, and one more consistent with probability and the general teachings of the Scriptures themselves put in their place; some of which will be presented in the next chapter.

CHAPTER VII.

THE DYNASTIC THEORY, OR A LONG CHRONOLOGY, IN HARMONY WITH THE GENERAL TEACHINGS OF THE BIBLE.

I. THE Bible, outside of the places in dispute, as I have already said, nowhere assigns a great age to individual men, but contains passages opposed to such an idea. I am now prepared to say that it never assigns a short term of existence to the human race, but, on the contrary, has various passages implying a long one, both before and after the flood.

1*st*, The "six days of creation," mentioned in the first chapter of Genesis, as now universally understood, stand for six successive epochs, or great cycles of time. Hence, if the first chapter calls a geological epoch after a day, the fifth chapter of the same book, to be consistent in style, should call a dynastic epoch after its founder; or, in other words, if a day become an epoch without changing its name, so a man may become a nation without changing his. As scholars now add the epochs together to ascertain the age of the earth, so in like manner we should add the dynasties together to ascertain the age of man upon it. If the first chapter describe a series of material changes of vast duration, why should not the fifth chapter describe a series of political changes of vast duration also? The first six chapters are but a *multum in parvo* of what transpired between the creation and the flood. The field of the record was so wide, the time so long, the objects so many, and the conditions so varied, that a hint was made to stand for an explanation, a day for an epoch, an individual for a race, a species for a genus, a father for a family, a chief for a nation, and a type or symbol for things of a moral and spiritual character. Evening, morning, day, night, herb, tree, fish, fowl, cattle, beast, serpent, Adam, Eve, Cain, Seth, Enos, and many others that might be mentioned, all seem to partake more or less of such peculiarity in the first chapters of Genesis.

2*nd*, In the fourth chapter, Cain's line is run to within two generations of Noah, and it is there said that Jabal, Jubal and Tubal-Cain were the fathers or progenitors of such tribes or nations as had become distinguished for cattle-raising, music, and the mechanical arts prior to the five hundredth year of

Noah. These nations are spoken of in the present tense,* as if then in existence and the contemporaries of the writer himself. For the descendants of the last named of the line to accomplish all this, and become so different in their respective habits of life, require far more time, it seems to me, than can possibly be gotten out of two generations of men—at least 1,277 years, or the lives of Lamech and Noah together, considered as consecutive dynasties. If this be correct, then how many years would it take to carry us back to Cain, their great ancestor?

3rd, As heretofore said, the first nine verses of the sixth chapter return to the "days when men began to multiply upon the earth," and pass rapidly over nearly the whole interval covered by the table in the fifth. They have, as every one can perceive, a very ancient flavor, and require long ages to thoroughly fill the measure of their demands. At a very early day the sons of God intermarried with the daughters of men; the giants, or great chiefs, lived in or before "those days;" for, "after that," the offspring of these marriages found time to become the "mighty men, who were of *old* the men of renown." If these latter persons were the ancients,

* "Such as *dwell* in tents, and *handle* the harp."

or the men of old, to the author one hundred years prior to the flood, how far into the past would it send the "giants," or great chiefs, who had, apparently, flourished and passed away before the first of them were born? Does not the reader feel that such language demands the most of the 7,737 years appropriated by me to the antediluvian period of the world?

4*th*, The deep rooted, universal, and terrible corruption attributed to the race at that time, together with the exhausted patience of a long-suffering and merciful God, conspire together in testifying that ages on ages had been devoted to the rise, growth, and maturity of such extreme wickedness.

II. This section will be devoted to the period between the deluge and the birth of Abraham, or the departure of his father Terah from Ur of the Chaldees.

1*st*, The tenth chapter of Genesis is a universal history or general outline of what the descendants of Noah had accomplished prior to the "division of the land" in the days of Peleg, the point where the account closes.

From the nature and magnitude of the things accomplished we may infer the length of the interval.

The first paragraph says: "Now these are the generations of the sons of Noah: Shem, Ham, and Japheth; and to them were sons born after the flood. The sons of Japheth: Gomer, Magog, Madai, Javan, Tubal, Meshech, and Tiras. The sons of Gomer: Ashkenaz, Riphath, and Togarmah. The sons of Javan: Elishah, Tarshish, Kittim, and Dodanim. By these"—or rather the descendants of these—"were the isles of the Gentiles divided in their lands; every one after his tongue, after their families, in their nations." The thing to observe here is the fact that, by the days of Peleg, the posterity of Japheth had spread themselves from Scythia to Spain,* had gotten possession of all the islands or maritime regions along the northern coast of the Mediterranean Sea, and already become separated into different "languages, families, and *nations*." What ages must have been consumed in producing these results! They are not those of leaps, bounds, or miracles, but the steady operations of natural causes.

The second paragraph says: "The sons of Ham: Cush, Mizraim, Phut, and Canaan. The sons of Cush: Seba, Havilah, Sabtah, Raamah, and Sab-

* See Josephus.

techah. The sons of Raamah: Shebah, and Dedan. And Cush begat Nimrod"—that is, was the ancestor of Nimrod. "He began to be a mighty one in the earth. He was a mighty hunter (conqueror) before the Lord. Wherefore it is said, Even as Nimrod the mighty conqueror before the Lord. And the beginning of *his kingdom* was Babel, and Erech, and Accad, and Calneh, in the land of Shinar. Out of that land he went forth into Asshur (Assyria) and builded Nineveh, the city of Rehoboth, Calah, and Resen, between Nineveh and Calah; the same is a great city." See what the Cushite branch of the Hamitic family have accomplished; what a mighty empire they have established apparently by conquest; what a number of great walled cities they have built; and what a reputation Nimrod, one of their emperors, has obtained, all before the end of Peleg's day. I need not quote the doings of Mizraim and Canaan, the founders of the ancient kingdoms of Egypt and Phoenecia, for all the sons of Ham have before that date become "families, tongues, countries, and nations."

Paragraph third says: "Unto Shem also, the father of all the children of Heber, the brother of Japheth the elder (of the two), even to him were children born. The children of Shem: Elam, Asshur, Arphaxad, Lud, and Aram. And the children of Aram: Uz, Hul, Gether, and Mash." These have also become distinct nations in their respective countries. Arphaxad was the "chosen" son of Shem. His family settled in the land of Ur, below the junction of the Tigris and the Euphrates, and became the Chaldees. "And Arphaxad begat Salah, and Salah begat Heber. And unto Heber were born two sons; the name of one was Peleg; for in his days the *land was divided*"—that is, the confederacy of the chosen people was divided. His elder brother, Joktan, taking off twelve tribes of it, established an independent nation between Mesha and Sephar, a mountainous region of the east; while Peleg's tribe remained in their original home, and continued the succession. How much this reminds us of the division of the kingdom of Israel between the rival houses of Judah and Ephraim, or their chiefs, Rehoboam and Jeroboam. The former, though retaining but two tribes, held the holy city, the temple, the law, and preserved the national life and religion; while the latter, taking off ten tribes, or the body of the nation, organized the semi-idolatrous kingdom of Samaria, which, after a few centuries, came to an end. Let this "division of the land" mean what it may, it occurred in the days of Peleg, and the important point is, that the tenth chapter gives the history of a grand series of events which all transpired previous to it—events which, from their very nature, seem to require the whole of the 1,867 years claimed by the dynastic scheme of interpretation.

Having thus prepared the way, let us now see how the matter stands.

The common mode of reckoning time is based on the Hebrew text as found in our English translation. It counts the figures as birth-dates, and allows only 131 years from the flood to the days of Peleg at the birth of his son Reu. The descendants of Noah, on the most liberal estimate, could not have then exceeded 900 persons, and the great majority of them would have been children.

How could they have divided into so many "families, tongues, and nations," settled in such distant portions of the earth, built great cities, and produced such a famous conqueror and monarch as Nimrod? Whence came the subjects of his kingdom? Another plan of reckoning is to follow the Samaritan text, which adds 100 years to the Hebrew in each case, making the sum of 531 years. This is much better than the other, but still falls far short of the time required for such grand results. The population descended from Noah could not have equalled one million of souls even at that date. Still another plan is to adopt the figures of the Septuagint version, which adds 200 years, and makes these patriarchs over 230 at the birth of their sons. But this is so forced, so unnatural, and so wanting in authority as to be unworthy of belief or attention.

If the names be taken as those of successive houses, then we shall have an interval between the flood and the "division of the land" of 1,867 years—not one year more, it seems to me, than the events of the tenth chapter of Genesis require.

I leave the intelligent reader to judge of this for himself, and proceed with the argument.

2nd. The eleventh chapter of Genesis does not begin its story where the tenth left off, but goes back to a point of time apparently very near to the deluge, to a time when the whole posterity of Noah formed only one community. The first nine verses of the chapter are confessedly obscure; the famous "confusion of tongues and dispersion of mankind," of which they speak, probably refer to the utter breaking up of the community or government of Noah, 350 years after the flood, the time when he is said to have died (Chap. ix. 28). At all events, these things can be readily explained in the following manner:

As the patriarchal names were also dynastic titles, the man Noah, who built the ark, was neither the first nor the last of his house; perhaps he was the eighth, as he is so styled in 2 Peter ii. 5. We must suppose the length of his life corresponded to that of his ancestors, and we therefore put it down at 180 years, 130 before and 50 after the flood. We would divide it thus, because his son Shem was then 100 years old, and because it is reasonable to reckon him about thirty years younger than his father.

Thus Noah, the builder of the ark, was the patriarch or head of the house for fifty years subsequent to the flood. On his death-bed he would naturally hand it over, *title and all,* to his eldest son,* whose family retained it for the next 300 years. Now, during those 350 years "the whole earth was of one

---

* Ham, we infer, as the curse fell on his house through Canaan, most probably his eldest son and representative. "*Younger son*" —Gen. ix. 24—refers to Canaan.

language and one speech"—that is, of one mind, one heart, and one enthusiasm. "And it came to pass, as they journeyed from the east, that they found a plain in the land of Shinar, and they dwelt there. And they said one to another, Come on, let us make brick, and burn them thoroughly, and let us build us a city, and a tower whose top may reach unto heaven; and let us make us a name, lest we be scattered abroad upon the face of the whole earth." The wording shows that they were possessed with a burning zeal for concentration and union, a zeal carried beyond the bounds of reason. "And the Lord came down to see the city and the tower which the children of men builded. And the Lord said, The people is one, and they have all one language (or purpose), and this they begin to do; and now nothing will be restrained from them, which they have imagined to do. Go to, let us go down and confound their language, that they may not understand (or give heed to) one another's speech. So the Lord scattered them abroad from thence upon the face of all the earth. And they left off to build the city. Therefore is the name of it called Babel; because the Lord did there confound the language of all the earth; and from thence did the Lord scatter them abroad upon the face of all the earth."

Thus fell the union; and thus fell the dynasty or government of Noah, after a long and glorious reign of 950 years. Here bursts the first grand mania of the new world. They undertook a task too great for their ability. After the cooling down of their first enthusiasm, they divided into different parties and opinions, as to the manner of conducting the work, till, falling into a general quarrel, in which one would not listen to the language or proposals of another, they finally broke up in utter confusion.

The heads of the several parties or tribes now led forth their adherents, and by degrees established themselves in the surrounding regions, where they became the various "families, tongues and nations" mentioned in the tenth chapter of Genesis.

The family of Arphaxed settled in the vicinity of the Persian Gulf, and became the great Chaldean nation, having the "sacred city of Ur for its capital," according to Mr. George Rawlinson and other writers."

3rd. The age of Shem is nowhere given; but the table beginning with chapter xi. 10, goes back and counts time from his birth, 100 years before the flood. Taking this view of the question, Shem and family were 150 years subject to the government of Noah, his father, 300 to the government of his eldest brother (ruling under the title of Noah till the fall of the house at the dispersion from Babel), and 150 as an independent community; in all, 600 years, when the house of Shem was succeeded by that of the chosen Arphaxad. Thus—

To the house of Shem (after the flood) are assigned 502 years.
" " Arphaxad are assigned . . 438 "
" " Salah " " . . 433 "
" " Heber " " . . 464 "
" " Peleg " " . . 239 "
" " Reu " " . . 239 "
" " Serug " " . . 230 "
" " Nahor " " . . 148 "
" " Terah in Ur " " . . 70 "

2,763 "

At this time another historic epoch occurred. The patriarch Terah broke up, at the command of God, and departed, with his infant son Abraham, from the ancient seat of the family, in Ur of the Chaldees, to go into the land of Canaan. For some reason he tarried by the way in the region of Haran, where he finally died, at the age of 145 years, as says the Samaritan text, which is undoubtedly the correct one in this particular. Then Abraham arose, being 75 years old, and came into the land of Canaan.

4th. The kingdom of Nimrod must have flourished prior to the "division of the land in the days of Peleg," yet long after the futile attempt to build the city and tower of Babel; for, though the "confusion" broke up the work on the *wall* and *tower*, and gave name to the place, it still became a *city* before the time of Nimrod, as we see from Gen. x. 10, 11, 12. There it is said, "The beginning of his kingdom was Babel, Erech, Accad and Calneh, in the land of Shinar," as if those cities were in existence before he took possession of them, while it is immediately added that he went out of that land into Asshur and *builded* Nineveh, Rehoboth, Calah, and Resen." This kingdom of Nimrod was doubtless the *first* Cushite monarchy in Babylonia, but not the last.

5th. There are also certain other statements and circumstances mentioned in Genesis which give unmistakable evidence of much more than 367 years from the deluge to Abraham's entrance into Canaan. Gen. xii. 6, says: "And Abram passed through the land unto the place of Sichem, unto the plain of Moreh; and *the Canaanite was then in the land.*"

We know from this, and various other allusions, that the inhabitants were then very numerous, and dwelling in walled towns; that the cities of Sodom, Gomorrah, Admah, Zeboim, Belah, &c., were capitals of Canaanitish States, with their kings residing in them; that these had been for twelve years tributary to Chedorlaomer, king of Elam, who was also confederate with three others reigning in the distant regions of the Euphrates; and that they were then sufficiently powerful to push their conquests westward to the plain of the Jordan, "Mount Seir, and the wilderness" of Arabia.

We also know that the Canaanitish people had already reached their full development, and were beginning to enter on that stage of decline which invariably follows idolatry and corruption of morals. The cup of iniquity of the cities in the plain was already full to the brim, and God, in His wrath, overthrew them with fire and brimstone from heaven. For them to have become so exceedingly corrupt and lascivious, we infer that they must have been very old, wealthy and luxurious communities long before that fearful destruction which was witnessed by the eyes of Abraham himself.

When then, we ask, did the descendants of Canaan

settle in Palestine and give their name to it? In what force did they come, and what was its condition on their arrival? We know it was not a wilderness, but occupied by the numerous tribes of the Rephaims, Zuzims, Emims, and others. Where did they come from, when did they arrive, and how long had they dwelt there before being dispossessed by the Canaanites? These are some of the questions which must be satisfactorily answered by those who contend that the chronology of the Hebrew Scriptures is short. Lenonnant and Chevalier, earnest Christian men, in their recent most excellent Manual of Ancient History, say: "Palestine when entered by the Canaanites, 2,400 or 2,300 B. C., was not a wilderness. The greater part of its towns were already built, and the country around them inhabited by a numerous population called the Rephaim, who were either exterminated or forced to emigrate by the Canaanites."

Mr. George Rawlinson, in his Ancient Monarchies, says: "The establishment of a Cushite kingdom in lower Babylonia dates probably from, at least, the twenty-fourth or twenty-fifth century before our era."* That is, four or five hundred years before

---

* Not under Nimrod, but a later one, I suppose.

the birth of Abraham, or the removal of Terah from Ur of the Chaldees. Further on he also says, that "these Cushites appear to have been a colony which came by sea, and whose conquests in Babylonia were followed rapidly by a Semitic emigration from the country—an emigration which took a northerly direction. The Assyrians withdrew from Babylonia, which they still always regarded as their parent land, and occupying the upper non-alluvial portion of the Mesopotamian plain, commenced the building of great cites in the tract upon the middle Tigris. The Phoenecians, or Canaanites, removed from the shores of the Persian Gulf, and, journeying towards the northwest, formed settlements upon the coast of Canaan, where they became a rich and prosperous people. The family of Abraham, and probably other Aramean ones, ascended the Euphrates, withdrawing from a yoke which was oppressive, or, at any rate, unpleasant. Abundant room was thus made for the Cushite emigrants, who rapidly established their preponderance over the whole of the southern region."

The quotations from these learned authors are substantially sustained by statements found in the book of Genesis and other early portions of the

Bible, and there are several ways of approximating the length of time which must have elapsed between the flood and Abraham's entrance into Canaan.

1*st*, If the Canaanites, on arriving there, five or six centuries before him, found the land "not a wilderness, but the greater part of its towns already built, and the country round about them inhabited by a numerous population of Rephaim and other tribes, it is evident that these original inhabitants must have found time, either there or elsewhere, to become a "strong and numerous people."

2*nd*, The early Cushites must have been members of the community which attempted to build the city and tower of Babel. After the "dispersion," they seem to have settled on the upper Nile and along the borders of the Red Sea, where they finally became a powerful nation, at least powerful enough to send off a colony by water in sufficient force to drive both the Elamite and Canaanite inhabitants from the regions of lower Babylonia and the Persian Gulf, about 2,500 B. C., or 500 years before the birth of Abraham.

3*rd*, When "Abraham went down into Egypt to sojourn," because of the famine in Canaan, he came in contact with "Pharaoh and his princes," and found the country flourishing under a regularly organized government, with a powerful priesthood at the head of an elaborate religious ritual. Hieroglyphic writing had long been in existence, and some of its largest pyramids standing both as monuments and silent witnesses of its great wealth, power, and antiquity. All these things, taken together, presuppose, not four centuries only, but the whole of the 2,763 years claimed in this work.

But some may say the flood was partial, being a punishment inflicted on the people of God then dwelling in the land of Eden, and should not be understood as destroying the inhabitants in other parts of the world. Very well. Both the truth and force of this objection may be fully admitted, but it will not at all help the matter; for all the mighty achievements above referred to, except those of the Rephaim tribes, were performed by the descendants of Noah himself, and it would have required more time and force for their accomplishment in populous regions than in vacant ones.

4*th*, The posterity of the patriarch Noah was, according to Genesis itself, most evidently very great on Abraham's entrance into Canaan; but according to the received mode of reckoning the table of the Hebrew text, it was only 367 years after the flood. Now, calculating the population on the same principles as was done in the case of Adam, it then consisted of less than 30,000 souls, a sum not equal, I suppose, to a third of the inhabitants of the one city of Sodom! This sum multiplied into itself, or 900,000,000, will very probably come much nearer the truth. Even China was then full of people.

5*th*, And in general, let us take the perception of David as to the number of generations which had passed prior to his day. He composed a historical psalm, to be sung on the happy occasion "when the Ark of God was brought from Obed-edom, and set in the midst of the tent which he had prepared for it." It is found both in the sixteenth chapter of 1st Chronicles, and also in the one hundred and fifth Psalm, with some verbal differences. I understand the Psalmist as recounting the dealings of God with His people from the beginning of the world down to his own times. He says—Ps. cv., 1 to 11— "O give thanks unto the Lord; call upon His name: make known His deeds among the people. Sing unto Him, sing psalms unto Him: talk ye of all His wondrous works. Glory ye in His holy name: let the heart of them rejoice that seek the Lord. Seek the Lord, and His strength: seek His face evermore. Remember the marvelous works that He hath done; His wonders, and the judgments of His mouth; O ye seed of Abraham His servant, ye children of Jacob His chosen. He is the Lord our God: His judgments are in all the earth. *He hath remembered His covenant for ever, the word which He commanded to a thousand generations.* Which He made (ratified) with Abraham: and His oath unto Isaac; and confirmed the same unto Jacob for a *law*, and to Israel for an *everlasting* covenant."

The Psalmist, it seems to me, here goes back in mind, like St. Paul in Hebrews xi., and looks upon the Lord as having remembered or kept His covenant of mercy and the word of His law during all the past ages of man. These appear to him so long and many that he does not hesitate to call them a "thousand generations." Though not to be taken literally, but poetically, both the conception and the language are in the past tense, and far too grand for the fourteen generations between Abraham and himself. Even poetry cannot call fourteen a thousand. He must then have counted them from the beginning of God's "judgments, covenants, promises, and commands to the children of men." On the authority of the Apostle Paul we know that, by faith in the covenant and promises of God, the "Elders, or ancient worthies, obtained a good report." "By that faith Abel offered unto God a more excellent sacrifice than Cain; Enoch was translated that he should not see death; Noah, being warned of God, prepared an ark to the saving of his house, condemned the world, and became heir of the righteousness which is by faith; and Abraham, when he was called to go out into a place which he should after receive for an inheritance, obeyed and went out, not knowing whither he went," &c. See Heb. xi.

David regarded the word and promises which the Lord had given and remembered for a thousand generations, as ratified with Abraham, as renewed with an oath to Isaac, as confirmed unto Jacob for a law, and to Israel for an *everlasting covenant.* From this last point his thought embraced the future, and not when he mentioned the covenant in connection with the name of Abraham; for if so, would there not be a glaring tautology in the language?

Now, there are only thirty-four generations from David to Adam, according to the third chapter of Luke, and even these are far too few to be called a thousand, under any kind of license whatever.

Then, if my view of the psalm be correct—and of this every one can judge for himself—David conceived of the human race as having existed at least as long as that for which I am contending.

I am now through with my argument from the Bible, and the conclusion to which I come is, that a short race-life, as well as a long individual-life, are both alike foreign to the Hebrew Scriptures. Their authors seem never to have dreamed of such ideas, but everywhere take the reverse for granted. Hence all objections to them on such grounds are wholly gratuitous, and made in ignorance of their contents. To reject the Bible, or any other grave book, without studying it, is, to say the least, unscholarlike, and can never secure the respect of thoughtful men.

The prevailing notions of the Jews on the subjects of patriarchal life and chronology cannot be shown to have existed, I suppose, previous to the Babylonish captivity. Theirs, like ours, have grown out of a misunderstanding of the tables in Genesis. These, since the captivity, have been as dead to them as to us, while their sources of information were never equal to ours of the present day. Moreover, it is perfectly plain, from their Talmud and other writings, that they are peculiarly inclined to misinterpret their own sacred books. Notwithstanding all this, Christians have, till very recently, simply followed their lead in these matters. But times are now changing, and as we have been compelled to abandon their views of the six days of creation, so we shall also be compelled to abandon their views of Scripture life and chronology.

CHAPTER VIII.

ARGUMENT FROM HISTORY.

I. HISTORY shows that man has been long on the earth, and in several ways corroborates our scheme of Scripture chronology.

1*st*, As the six successive epochs of creation, and the nineteen successive periods of human history in the book of Genesis, have each an appropriate name, so the twenty-five imperial houses or dynasties of China have each an appropriate name also—a resemblance which is very striking and suggestive.

Manetho also gives specific numbers to his thirty-one Egyptian dynasties which serve the purpose of names; while Berosus gives both names and numbers to his Babylonian kingdoms. Such, it would seem, has always been the course pursued by historians; for they instinctively arrange their epochs, periods, and dynasties according to their relations in time. They also name, number, epitomize, and tabulate them after a common mental law; and by the light of this law all such documents must be read and interpreted; and,

PATRIARCHAL DYNASTIES. 125

2*nd*, Every one will be struck with the fact, when he sees how the years under the several patriarchal names correspond to those of dynasties, empires, kingdoms, and special forms of government, in various nations of the world.

A comparison with some of the principal ones will make this correspondence sufficiently manifest.

HOUSE OR DYNASTY OF ADAM.

	Hebrew Text.	Samaritan Text.
Adam,	930 years,	930 years.
Seth,	912 "	912 "
Enos,	905 "	905 "
Cainan,	910 "	910 "
Mahalaleel,	895 "	895 "
Jared,	962 "	847 "
Enoch,	365 "	365 "
Methuselah,	969 "	720 "
Lamech,	777 "	653 "
Noah (to the flood),	600 "	600 "
Shem (after the flood),	502 "	502 "
Arphaxad,	438 "	438 "
Salah,	433 "	433 "
Heber,	464 "	404* "
Peleg,	239 "	239 "
Reu,	239 "	239 "
Serug,	230 "	230 "
Nahor,	148 "	148 "
Terah in Ur,	70 "	70 "
	10,988 "	10,440 "

Or, following the Samaritan text in the antediluvian, and the Hebrew in the postdiluvian tables, 10,500 "

* Supposed to be a clerical error for 464.

CHINESE DYNASTIES.*

Hea, . .	439 years.	Liang 2, . . 70 years.
Shang, . .	644 "	Ch'ân, . . 32 "
Cheu 2, . .	876 "	Sui, . . 30 "
T'sin, . .	40 "	T'ang 2, . . 300 "
Han 4, . .	474 "	Yuen, . . 88 "
Tsin 3, . .	173 "	Ming, . . 276 "
Sung 3, . .	320 "	T'sing, . . 232 "
T'si, . .	23 "	

EGYPTIAN DYNASTIES.

I., . .	253 years.	XVIII., . . 241 years.
II., . .	303 "	XIX., . . 174 "
III., . .	214 "	XX., . . 178 "
IV., . .	284 "	XXI., . . 130 "
V., . .	248 "	XXII., . . 170 "
VI., . .	203 "	XXIII., . . 89 "
VII.? . .	75 "	XXIV., . . 6 "
VIII., . .	142 "	XXV., . . 50 "
IX., . .	109 "	XXVI., . . 138 "
X., . .	185 "	XXVII., . . 121 "
XI. and XII.,	213 "	XXVIII., . . 7 "
XIII., .	453 "	XXIX., . . 21 "
XIV., .	184 "	XXX., . . 38 "
XV. XVI. XVII.,	511 "	XXXI. . . 8 "

Ended 339 B. C.

ASSYRIAN EMPIRES.

I., . . . 526 years.   II., . . . 122 years.

* Those bearing the same title are thrown together.

THE BABYLONIAN DYNASTIES OF BEROSUS, AS RESTORED BY RAWLINSON.

I. Chaldean,	? years.	V. Arabian,	245 years.
II. Median,	234 "	VI. ?	526 "
III. ?	48 "	VII.	122 "
IV. Chaldean,	458 "	VIII.	87 "

JEWISH PERIODS.

The Pilgrimage,	545 years.	The House of Israel,	254 years.
The Judges,	400 "	The Captivity,	70 "
The House of David,	468 "	The Restoration,	590 "

ROMAN FORMS OF GOVERNMENT.

The Kingdom, 244 years.   The Republic, 481 years.
The Empire, 504 years.

FRENCH DYNASTIES.

Merovingian,	241 years.	Orleans line,	91 years.
Capetian,	341 "	Bourbon branch,	260 "
Valois branch,	107 "		

RUSSIAN DYNASTIES.

Romanoff, 41 years.   Holstein, 114 years.

GERMAN DYNASTIES.

Carlovingian,	119 years.	Luxemburg line,	129 years.
Saxon line,	105 "	Hapsburg "	205 "
Salic "	114 "	Lorraine "	134 "
Hohenstaufens,	170 "		

ENGLISH HOUSES.

Saxons,	190 years.	York,	24 years.
Danes,	50 "	Tudor,	118 "
Normans,	88 "	Stuart,	111 "
Plantagenets,	245 "	Hanover,	162 "
Lancaster,	62 "		

Choo Foo Tsz, a celebrated Chinese philosopher and historian of the twelfth century, has well remarked that, "In the revolutions of time human affairs are not stable more than two or three hundred years."

By examining the duration of the above governments, we will readily perceive that the patriarchal names, even when considered as those of dynasties, are still abreast of any that have ever existed. They were perhaps religious rather than political communities; and since religious organizations are the most permanent of all human institutions, this may be sufficient to account for their surpassing length.

The present royal family of China is believed, by competent judges, to have transmitted the throne without break, from father to son, longer than any other in the annals of history, showing a regular descent of 231 years.

Ordinarily breaks frequently occur; sons are

adopted, a brother, uncle, nephew, or some member of a collateral branch comes in to continue the government (sometimes more than once) before the final overthrow and change of title takes place. Tables have neither time nor space for these details; hence we frequently find the figures increasing with the brevity of the catalogue or the remoteness of the dynasties mentioned.

II. Some of the above named governments began in the remote depths of antiquity; but even beyond them appear the dim outlines of still more remote ones. For instance, at the beginning of the Hia, 2,205 B. C., China was occupied by aboriginal tribes, who brought tribute to its rulers. Then beyond the Hia were the "Five Sovereigns," with Fuh-he at their head, whose united reigns covered a space, according to Dr. Williams, of 647 years; according to Professor Kidd, of 1,164. The exact date of Fuh-he's reign cannot be fixed, but it is generally supposed to be in the neighbourhood of 3,000 B. C. Some traditions say his posterity reigned for fifteen generations, over a period of 17,787 years.

Still beyond him comes the "*Jin Wong*," or fabulous King of Men, whose dynasty lasted 45,000 years under nine brothers. In those days, says the story,

"The hills and rivers were divided into nine regions. The people occupied but one territory, observed respectful manners, and pure customs. The kingly office was not a pageantry, nor were the functions of state ministers empty titles. Good government was established by the rulers, and correct institutions diffused among the common people."

Again, this golden age was preceded by "*Te Wong*," or the King of the World, whose rule continued 18,000 years under eleven brothers. Prior to him was "*Tien Wong*," or the King of Heaven, who reigned 18,000 years; and still beyond him was "*Pwan Koo*," the first man, who spent 18,000 more years in "chiseling out the earth, cutting passages through the mountains, teaching navigation, and otherwise preparing it for the habitation of men."

These things, though fables, show plainly that the origin of the Chinese people lies concealed in the depths of a remote past. Such stories and dates would be unworthy of attention were it not for the fact that they contain shadowy glimpses of the governments and history of those lost ages. It will be a difficult task to convince intelligent Chinamen that man has existed no more than 6,000 years.

2*nd*, The Chaldean empire presents a similar

record. According to Rawlinson, the *Second Dynasty* began 2,286 B. C. He says: "Berosus declared that six dynasties had reigned in Chaldea since the great flood of Xisuthrus, or Noah. To the first, consisting of eighty-six kings, he allowed the extravagant period of 34,080 years. Evechous, its founder, had enjoyed the royal dignity for 2,400, and Chomasbelus, his son and successor, 300 longer than his father. The other eighty-four kings had filled up the remaining space of 28,980 years, their reigns thus averaging 345 apiece."

Unfortunately the works of Berosus have been lost; only a mutilated outline of his chronological scheme being preserved to us through extracts by Eusebius, and one or two others. It is clear that something is wrong with the numbers above given. Through frequent transcription, they may have become dislocated; for they seem to bear marks of this on their face. I venture to suggest that the 34,080 years were meant to cover the period *before* the flood of Xisuthrus, 2,400 years, and the eighty-six kings that of the *first Chaldean* dynasty *after* it.*
This would require an average reign of only twenty-

---

* This was probably the kingdom of Nimrod.

eight years for each of these kings, which is clearly within the bounds of reason.

Then, on this supposition, if we add the 2,400 years to the 2,286 B. C., the commencement of the second dynasty, we shall have 4,686 B. C. for the great flood of Xisuthrus. The date of Noah's flood, according to our scheme of interpreting the tables of Genesis, is 4,763 B. C., leaving a difference between the two dates of only seventy-seven years, which is a fraction of no importance in a question of this kind. Berosus certainly regarded men as having dwelt a long time in the region of Babylonia, both before and after the flood; but as I have not his "fragments" at hand, I touch on the matter with great reserve, and beg not to be held responsible for any errors which may have crept into my remarks.

Modern researches in the valley of the Euphrates tend to confirm the truth of Berosus' convictions. The account of the flood, recently found at Nineveh, was translated from a *dead language* into the cuneiform character for the library of Sardanapalus, according to the opinion of Mr. Smith, the distinguished Assyrian scholar. The story, even in the original, had become highly mythological, which is an unmistakable sign of great age.

3rd, Both the history and monuments of Egypt give proof of the highest antiquity. On any theory of explaining Manetho's thirty-one dynasties, it is very high. M. Lenormont, regarding them as all consecutive, fixes the date of the first at 5,004 B. C. Baron Bunsen, regarding them as mostly consecutive, fixes it at 3,643 B. C. Mr. Poole, maintaining that they were largely contemporaneous, puts it at 2,717 B. C. Even after every effort to bring them within the bounds of the received Scripture chronology, he is compelled to place their beginning 425 years prior to Usher's deluge.

The "'List of Kings' recently discovered in the Temple of Abydos, represents Seti I, accompanied by his son Rameses II, in the act of paying homage to seventy-six of his ancestors, beginning with Menes." Now, the end of the reign of Rameses is fixed by Egyptologists at about 1,340 B. C. By allowing twenty-three years as the average reign of each of these seventy-six kings of Egypt, and multiplying the two together, the sum of 1,748 years will be produced, which, added to the 1,340 B. C., will place Menes, the head of the first dynasty, at 3,088

B. C. Again, if the seventy-five ancestors of Christ, given in the third chapter of Luke, cover a period of 4,004 years, certainly the seventy-six ancestors of Rameses should do the same; and this would send Menes full 3,000 years beyond Usher's flood. I however regard Bunsen's date as decidedly preferable to all others; and I have also seen it frequently stated that the most recent discoveries in Egypt tend to confirm it. We thus see that our scheme of Scripture chronology exactly meets the wants of the case, by placing the flood 1,120 years beyond Bunsen's date, which allows Menes sufficient time to be the descendant of Noah, and the founder of a State on the banks of the Nile.

Manetho, notwithstanding the very high point to which he carried the history of Egypt, still believed that kingdoms flourished long previous to the reign of Menes, as he assigns 12,843 years to "heroes and the gods." He was not so wide of the mark after all, it would seem, as the Bible is now shown to supply 8,857 of them, counting from Bunsen's date.

4*th*, I need only mention the belief among the people of India of many eras of human existence, the last of which began 3,100 years before the birth of Christ.

CHAPTER IX.

ARGUMENT FROM SCIENCE, TRADITION, AND MYTHOLOGY.

OUR fathers, only a few centuries ago, accepted less than 6,000 years as the term of human existence without the least misgiving; but modern researches in various departments of history and science have exploded this opinion, and put in its place some vast indefinite number. This may be farther from the truth than that which it has supplanted. Yet it cannot be less than the 14,376 years above claimed, as I shall still proceed to show.

1st. Argument from Geology.

The argument from geology may be briefly stated thus: It holds that, during the ages which have already run their rounds in connection with our earth, a long lease of life has been allotted to each of the many extinct species of animals, but comparatively only a very short one to separate individuals. The inference is, that such has been the case with man also.

Again, "the present rate of deposition on the earth's surface must be taken as the normal or standard rate for the recent formations." Now, human remains and implements have been found in great abundance in beds of gravel and other deposits, associated with animal bones, under such conditions as to make it impossible to suppose that they had been there less than 14,000 years. Many say much more.

2nd. Argument from Archaeology.

Of late years great attention has been given to this department, and most interesting discoveries have been made in almost every portion of the globe. The mounds and other monuments that man has left behind him are acknowledged on all hands to be most hoary with age; so much so, that Mr. Bancroft does not hesitate to attribute to some of those found in America even "thousands of ages." I have seen them in great numbers myself, and I feel safe in saying that the Mississippi valley must have been inhabited in very ancient times by a powerful and civilized people. If the Chinese race should be swept away, they would not leave behind them monuments equal in size and workmanship to those of America.

3rd. Argument from Ethnology.

Ethnology maintains the unity of mankind, and requires fully as much time as my theory claims to bring all its varying tribes and races back to a common ancestry. It holds that the three most strongly marked races are exceedingly tenacious of their distinguishing characteristics—the negro having undoubtedly remained unchanged for the last 3,000 years, with the fair inference of three times that amount.

4th. Argument from Philology.

Philology teaches that languages are of slow growth, and, like the races of man, are also very tenacious of their own peculiarities; that the differences existing among them are very great, and known to have been so from the beginning of the historic age. Yet they all, whether monosyllabic, agglutinate, or amalgamate, present certain features in common which prove, or strongly suggest, a common origin. Many of them rose, flourished, and passed away before the Christian era; while those which now prevail retain certain "survivals," or fossil forms and significations, indicative of a long career. In words are found the most ancient of human remains; and though it is impossible to assign to their origin any definite date, it must, beyond all doubt, be put very high in order to meet the requirements of the case.

Baron Bunsen claims for the origin, growth, and divisions of language a term of 20,000 years. Prof. Whitney, and other philologists, still more. No one, I venture to say, with even a tolerable knowledge of the subject, can believe that they were all one under 14,000 years ago. The Chinese language has a history of its own covering a third of that time; and we may well ask, when were the English, Greek, and other amalgamates the same with it? If these wide differences were produced by a sudden "confusion of tongues" at the building of the Tower of Babel, then that event must be placed a great way off. But if it was, as some maintain, not a confusion of *articulation*, but a confusion of *talk*—a grand quarrel that broke up the work, and caused the dispersion so graphically described in the eleventh chapter of Genesis, then it did not directly affect the course of linguistic development. Let this question be decided as it may, it matters not as to the subject in hand, for philology says it has been a very great while since all the languages of the world were the same.

5*th*. Argument from Tradition.

The traditions found in Babylonia, Egypt, China, India, and elsewhere, all point to the unity and remote origin of the human race.

In studying these traditions we should remember that associated objects, when viewed from a distance, lose their identity and blend into one. So the doings of a whole nation or age may become associated with the name of some prominent individual, striking emblem, or national soubriquet, and thus embodied, be handed down to future generations.

In this way, the whole history of England may, in the progress of ages, when some "New Zealander shall stand on the ruins of London bridge," and try to decipher the past from bits of stone, be ascribed to an ancient giant called John Bull. His wife, Britannia, may then be the goddess of the sea, and their son, Jonathan, the Hero or Hercules of North America. Then their temples, statues, and worship may prevail through all the present Anglo-Saxon portions of the globe. But we hope for better things in the future. When events become too grand, numerous, and complicated in their relations for the ready grasp of the mind, it begins instinctively to concentrate, individualize, or personify them; and thus the stories of the creation of the world, the fall of man, the flood, the long life, and wonderful exploits of certain ones of the olden times, show clearly that they lived in ages far away, fully far enough for nations to become individual men, for men to become giants, heroes, and gods, before the dawn of authentic history.

Thus we see that these traditions, when properly considered, also join their testimony with the other witnesses in supporting our views of Biblical chronology.

6*th*. Argument from Mythology or Religion.

Mythology or religion, as a science, treats of the fundamental ideas of the human race, together with the various systems which they have produced. At first these ideas, according to the most ancient records and evidences, were monotheistic. But peoples, in their migrations from their central home and worship, met with wars, floods, earthquakes, famines, pestilences, and other trying conditions. These developed leaders of remarkable wisdom, skill, virtue, or prowess. The people, seeing these, gradually, but naturally, gave personality to the forces able to produce such results; clothed them with Divine attributes; associated with them the creations of their own excited imaginations; and so finally made them images, shrine sand temples; adopted in their honor certain observances and rites, which imperceptibly multiplied and grew into all the various systems of false worship found among men.

In this way mythology becomes a record of facts, and, to some extent, contains within it the history and chronology of the race.

Nothing human is so slow of growth, and so slow of decay, as religious systems. Now Monotheism, the original form of worship, had arisen, flourished, and decayed; then Polytheism had succeeded to it, and grown into full blast in Babylonia, Egypt, and China, all before our first acquaintance with those nations.

"The religion of Chaldea," says Mr. Rawlinson, "from the earliest times to which the monuments carry us back, was, in its outward aspect, a Polytheism of a very elaborate character. Various deities, whom it was not considered at all necessary to trace to a single stock, divided the allegiance of the people, and even of the kings, who regarded with equal respect, and glorified with equally exalted epithets, some fifteen or sixteen different personages. Next to these principal gods were a far more numerous assemblage of inferior or secondary ones, less often mentioned, and esteemed as less worthy of honor, but still recognized generally through the country." "Finally," says he, "the Pantheon contained a host of mere local gods or genii, every town, and almost every village of Babylonia being under the protection of its own particular divinity. But it would be impossible to give a complete account of this vast and complicated system. The subject is still but partially worked out by cuneiform scholars, and the difficulties in the way of understanding it are very great."

Not only so; both the "Book of Funeral Rites," and all the monuments of Egypt, declare the same thing as to the state of religion in the region of the Nile, at the remotest date to which students have been able to go.

In China, the system of ancestral worship, even during the Cheu dynasty, which began 1,122 B. C., was most elaborate and minute, being as thoroughly crystalized at that time as at the present day.

It will not be necessary to speak of the religions of India, Greece, Mexico, Peru, and other ancient nations, as they all seem to have passed through very similar stages.

In view of such facts, may we not most confidently hold that thousands of years must have been required for the primitive Monotheism to die out, and these varied systems of Polytheism to rise, develop, and become elaborate and complicated, even crystalized, in nations so many and remote from each other?

Lastly, though physiology is silent as to the age of the race, it is not so as to the length of individual life—which is an essential part of this discussion—and, therefore, it may also come forward with its testimony.

Physiology treats of the organs of animal life, their functions, growth, and decay. The laws governing these things, so far as ascertained, seem to forbid the idea that men were ever able to live beyond two hundred years. Generally, in less than half that time, the vital organs lose their vigor, the best eyes become blind, the best ears deaf, and the best teeth that ever grew worn down to the roots. Then, unless we suppose some wonderful change to have taken place in the material or construction of our bodies, those glorious old antediluvian patriarchs would have been over six or seven hundred years of their lives "sans eyes, sans ears, sans teeth, sans everything," burdens to themselves, and objects of pity to their people!

Familiarity with an idea does a great deal towards reconciling us to it, but it is *in reality* as easy for us to conceive of men extraordinarily large as of men extraordinarily old. Let us now present the proposition to ourselves in this unfamiliar manner, and see what will be the result. It is a simple question of proportion. We will take ninety years as the age of men now, and six feet as their height. Then as ninety is to nine hundred and thirty, the age of Adam, so is six feet to his height, equal to sixty-two feet!. Keeping up the symmetry of his person, his waist was thirty odd feet around, and his foot eight feet long—requiring one hundred yards of cloth for a suit of clothes, four ox hides for a pair of boots, and a wagon load of provisions for a dinner!! If such were the ordinary men of "those days," what were the "giants?"*

I here close my arguments with the profound conviction that our venerable Scriptures furnish a solid foundation on which we may rest in regard to the

* Double the ordinary size, age, weight, or strength, would be marvelous, much beyond that, supernatural. Eleven feet is the highest man of whom I have any reliable information.

age of man, both as individuals, and as a race. Though my scheme of interpretation may not be entirely free from difficulties and mistakes, it is in the main correct, and can never be overthrown by bringing objections against particular parts; but it must stand or fall as a whole.

The argument is accumulative, one, and indivisible, having the verb *lived* for its pedestal.

Objections Answered.

The following objections are here given as specimens of those which may be brought against my scheme of interpretation:

1*st*, "Was the dynasty of Enoch translated?" By no means. Enoch, the head of the house, "walked with God" sixty-five years, when God took him; after which, his house, or regular successors, walked with God three hundred more, when it was succeeded by that of Methuselah. I see no special difficulty here.

2*nd*, "Did the whole dynasty of Noah enter the ark?" Not at all. Only the Noah who was its chief at the time of the flood.

3*rd*, "If the verb *lived* implies death, as used in the tables, then did not Terah die in Ur at seventy years of age, instead of in Haran?" Genesis xi. 26 to 32.

Answer. He *ceased to live in Ur* at that time. Only this first part of his life was on the registers of Ur. His headship terminated at seventy, which is all that is demanded of the verb.

4*th*, "Could scholars of every grade overlook all these things for so many ages, and such important truths remain concealed till discovered by yourself?" This objection makes truth a monopoly, stops all progress, and upholds every error that ever existed. It is scarcely worth a serious reply. Facts and arguments are everything in a question of this kind; authority nothing. Study has corrected many popular notions, and is destined to correct many more.

5*th*, "The Septuagint version supplies all the time required by established facts, and its dates are followed by many eminent men." I answer, it is wanting in authority, and produces more confusion in the main, if we count by births, then the Hebrew text. It relieves its adherents somewhat as to the duration of the race, but plunges them into inextricable difficulties in other respects.

6*th*, "The Bible does not pretend to furnish data for chronological purposes, and, therefore, every system based upon it is fallacious." I deny the assertion. Why, then, does it give a regular series of dates from Adam to the Captivity, or burden itself with so many figures?

7th, "The dynastic scheme, which allows only 14,376 years for the existence of man, fails to meet the case; for modern discoveries claim hundreds of thousands." I deny the claim. It is as yet an assumption only; the proof is still wanting. On the contrary, I assert that the 14,376 years fills every demand of history and science. Again, it should be remembered that the *chronology* of the Scriptures begins, not with the creation of man (chap. i. 27), but with *Adam, the father of Seth* (chap. v. 3.) All the history of the race prior to him, if any, is left dateless, and opens a question into which I have not pretended to enter. On this point, I wait for further light. Neither is it my province to reconcile the Bible with modern discoveries, but to show its teachings as to the ages of the ancient patriarchs, together with the period of time which elapsed between the father of Seth and the birth of Abraham. I have laboured to correct a general misapprehension as regards these two points alone, without turning aside to other things. Truths reconcile themselves.

8th, "The dynastic mode of interpretation is too complicated, and not in accordance with the first impression or obvious meaning of the language employed in the tables."

Answer. There is a dangerous fallacy in this familiar axiom. It holds good only of things in themselves plain or simple; but as to such complex matters as the creation, the flood, geology, astronomy, chronology, history, and the like, first impressions, obvious meanings, and popular opinions, are invariably wrong, and have to be corrected by a careful collection of facts, and scientific processes of reasoning. According to the obvious meaning of the record, the heavens and the earth were created in six ordinary days, the whole globe was submerged to the top of the highest mountains, and every living thing outside of the ark was drowned in Noah's flood. According to first impressions the sun rises and sets, the earth is flat or square; light and darkness, heat and cold, are equally forces of nature; but the learned know better.

When mountains seem to revolve, trees to walk, or men to live 1,000 years, we should at once suspect an optical illusion. Again, our scheme of chronology is not particularly complicated; not more so than the nature of the subject requires. It is only new and startling; a little familiarity with it will relieve the difficulty.

9*th*, "Could God have allowed the world of mankind to remain without the Saviour and the gospel for such a long time as twelve thousand five hundred years?"

ANSWER. On the same principles that He could leave it four thousand. Men have walked with God in all ages; He has never "left Himself without witness," and "is no respecter of persons; but in every nation and age he that feareth Him and worketh righteousness is accepted of Him." I have no means of satisfactorily answering this and many like questions, and I am, moreover, unable to see how they bear on points relating to matters of fact. To study the Bible not less, but history and the sciences more, might remove this class of difficulties from pious minds.

10*th*, To those infidels who object to the Bible because of the length of the patriarchal life and the shortness of its chronology, I would recommend this little book. After they have read it carefully, their respect for the Bible may increase, and they may feel more inclined to study it for themselves. If so, they will find it a very different book from what they have supposed, and be greatly benefitted by it.

Conclusion.

I here bring my labors to a close. I have studied and written in the interest of truth alone. I give the result to the public in the hope that it may profit all classes. It is only an outline of a vast picture. The filling up I leave to other and abler hands, to the mighty host of earnest workers now in the field.

Columbus showed us the New World, the Bible shows us the Old—and a grand Old World it is—with a history stretching across a space of at least ten thousand five hundred years.

In process of time, the nations contemporaneous with its patriarchal dynasties in all parts of the earth will come forth from their long sleep of oblivion, and take up their positions on the huge canvas with every limb and muscle standing out in bold relief, the heritage of future generations. May a rich reward await every one who aids in its completion.

APPENDIX.

THE following extract is taken from a review of Dr. Gustave Schlegel's recent great work on Chinese Uranography, published in the November-December number of the "Chinese Recorder and Missionary Journal," Shanghai, 1875:

"A sonorous title is perhaps a fit prelude to a remarkable book, and such we think the work before us may fairly claim to be. The gifted author is known by reputation to many China residents from his able contributions to the local periodicals. The present is no ephemeral production, being the outcome of continuous investigation, prolonged through a series of years. The object of the work may be stated in brief to be—to trace to their source the facts of Uranography, and to give some account of their *raison d' être.*"

Dr. Schlegel is not the first who has attempted an interpretation of the quaint figures with which western science has been pleased to tapestry the starry vault above our heads; but in the theory which he has put forward in elucidation, we believe he is quite original.

In developing this theory, it is very evident he has not been unduly influenced by consequences; but following it up to its legitimate result, he has arrived at the notable conclusion, that the names of the constellations on the Chinese sphere indicate an antiquity of nearly 17,000 years before the Christian era. Where all preceding theorists may be said to have failed, it is but fair that we should give a hearing to an authority of Dr. Schlegel's standing. We venture, therefore, to trace the steps by which he has arrived at this result; and preliminary to this we may state his four cardinal propositions:

1*st*, The names on our celestial globes, as derived from the Egyptians and Greeks, are, with some few exceptions, utterly inapplicable to the circumstances of the ancient nations to whom they have been generally attributed.

2*nd*, The names of the constellations on the Chinese sphere correspond exclusively to the condition of the Chinese.

3*rd*, Nearly all the names of the Chinese asterisms

being found on our western globes, they must have been borrowed from the Chinese by western nations, which have since added some new constellations of their own.

4*th*, The antiquity of Chinese Uranography is corroborated by the testimony of Chinese tradition and history, as also by the researches of European geologists.

The first of these propositions we may pass over without much misgiving; or at least take it for granted, and proceed to the consideration of the second. Here we are met by an anomaly at the outset, which has proved a sore puzzle to all Dr. Schlegel's predecessors. We may state it more intelligibly to Europeans by using our familiar signs of the zodiac rather than the Chinese names. Thus with us *Capricornus* represents the winter solstice, *Aries* the vernal equinox, *Cancer* the summer solstice, and *Libra* the autumnal equinox; corresponding in rotation with the north, west, south, and east.

The Chinese on the contrary are unanimously persistent in giving the rotation thus: *Capricornus* for winter—in the north; *Libra* for spring—in the west; *Cancer* for summer—in the south; and *Aries* for autumn—in the east.

This arrangement is no modern institution with the Chinese, for the very earliest astronomical notices they have handed down to us are in the same (to us) grotesque attitude. In the infancy of society, when they first began rudely to divide the sphere into four parts for the convenience of agriculture, these were termed Kucei, the "Tortoise," roughly covering our *Sagittarius*, *Capricornus* and *Aquarius*, and assigned to the north, or winter; Hou, the "Tiger," standing for *Pisces*, *Aries*, and *Taurus*, assigned to the east, or autumn; Neaou, the "Bird," for *Gemini*, *Cancer*, and *Leo*, assigned to the south, or summer; and Lung, the "Dragon," for *Virgo*, *Libra*, and *Scorpio*, assigned to the spring and the east.

It will be seen that the great difficulty here is, that while *Capricornus* and *Cancer* hold their natural positions, those of *Aries* and *Libra* are mutually reversed. As astronomical observations advanced, and each of these quarters became subdivided into seven parts, thus forming the zodiac of twenty-eight constellations, the same theory was still preserved, as it is to the present day. An able Sinalogue remarks on this question: "This discrepancy does not seem, however, to trouble the minds of the Chinese at all, and we may safely leave it unexplained."

Another indication of the signs of the seasons is found in the beginning of the *Shoo King*, one of the oldest Chinese documents extant. We read there that the emperor* (?) "commanded the second brother, *Ho*, to reside at the Bright Valley, and there respectfully to receive as a guest the rising sun, and to adjust and arrange the labors of the spring. *He said*, 'The star is in *Neaou;* you may thus exactly determine mid-spring.' * * * He further commanded the third brother, *Hie*, to reside at *Nan-keaou*, and arrange the transformation of the summer, and respectfully to observe the *extreme limit of the shadow*. * * * * *He said*, 'The star is *Ho;* you may thus exactly determine mid-summer.' He separately commanded the second brother, *Ho*, to reside at the West, and there respectfully to convoy the setting sun, and to adjust and arrange the completing labours of the autumn. *He said*, 'The star is *Heu;* you may thus exactly determine mid-autumn.' He further commanded the third brother, *Hie*, to reside in the northern region, and there to adjust and examine the changes of the winter. *He said*, 'The star is *Maou;* thus you may exactly determine mid-winter.'"

* *Yaou*, as heretofore supposed; but Dr. S. disputes this, and regards these commands as an ancient tradition.

In this extract we find the names of four stars given—*i. e.*, *Neaou, Ho, Heu,* and *Maou,*—or, substituting the more modern names for *Neaou* and *Ho,* we have *Sing, Fang, Heu,* and *Maou,* pointing out respectively the equinoxes and solstices. But how these stars indicate the terms in question—in what position or at what hour—has hitherto baffled all expositors, both native and foreign, satisfactorily to explain.

After a summary view of the various theories that have been proposed, Dr. Schlegel proceeds to expound his own, which amounts to something like this: The inadequacy of every scheme that has been proposed to make this legend synchronize with the reputed time of the Emperor *Yaou,* shows it to be not a contemporary record, but a tradition handed down from remote antiquity. As to the manner in which the four stars above named are to point out their respective terms, he professes to follow literally the guidance of *Yaou's* commission. At spring, the astronomer is told "respectfully to receive as a guest the rising sun," implying sunrise as the time for observation; at the autumn term, the orders are "respectfully to convoy the setting sun," implying sunset as the time of observation; mid-summer was to be determined by "the extreme length of the shadow," implying noon as the time of observation; and mid-winter was to be determined by the culmination of the star *Muou*, thus implying midnight as the time of observation. Having fixed on the mode of operation, it is obvious that the secular displacement of the seasons by precession, will not vitiate the theory; and it only remains to ascertain how the year stood in regard to the sidereal sphere, at the time the constellations were named. This Dr. Schlegel professes to have done by an elaborate and critical analysis of the names of all the asterisms known to Chinese astronomy.

The conclusion to which he is led by this investigation, is that the cradle of astral science was, in China, somewhere about the 35th degree of north latitude and that the star *Heu*, or β Aquarii, culminated at midnight on the winter solstice, and the star *Fang*, or π Scorpionis, consequently marked the vernal equinox.

By calculation he finds that when these events took place, the equinoctial colure intersected the equator about 250 degrees in arrear of its present position. The star *Fang* would then rise due east at 5 *a. m.* on the morning of the vernal equinox;

and *Maou*, or the Pleiades, would set with the sun, being consequently invisible, on the evening of the autumnal equinox. There is a curious phenomenon attendant on this position, which Dr. Schegel does not fail to press into his service; that is, on the vernal equinox in question, the star *x* Librae, which would rise with the sun, bears the Chinese name *Jih*, or the "sun" star; while A Tauri, that would set with the sun on the day of the autumnal equinox, bears the Chinese name of *Yue*, or the "*Maou* star."

The next step was to ascertain at what period the above phenomena took place, which is a simple question of calculating the precession of the equinoxes. Thus, 250 degrees = 90,000 seconds, which divided by 50,2563″ (the annual precession,) gives a quotient of 17,908 years, since the vernal equinox was in the neighborhood of Antares. But this is not all; for it is found that the precession is more rapid now than it was in the days of yore; which requires 808 years to be added to the above number, making altogether 18,716 years. Then deducting the eighteen centuries of the Christian era, the result will be 16,916 B. C. as the date of the foundation of Chinese Uranography. "We have thus endeavored," says the reviewer, "to give, as concisely as practicable, an outline of the system to the elucidation of which Dr. Schlegel has devoted some 940 quarto pages. The work is a perfect thesaurus of information regarding the astrology and astronomy of the ancients, illustrated by a profusion of interesting matter relating to the history, habits and customs of the Chinese. That he has brought a vast amount of learning to bear on his subject, is apparent to the most superficial reader; that he has discovered many curious facts, is beyond dispute; and that he has succeeded in pulling to pieces the various schemes that have been thought out for the explanation of the anomalies of Chinese astronomy is perfectly true; yet we confess the evidence adduced is of such a voluminous and complex character, that we have not gone over it with that care necessary to render a decided opinion of any great value."

The work is just issued, in French. Only that portion of the review which gives the contents is transcribed above, for the purpose of showing the kind of questions that constantly arise out of Chinese antiquities. I have myself formed no opinions as to the merits of Dr. Schlegel's theory, and, of course, am not responsible for those of the reviewer.

The following extract is taken from *"Littell's Living Age,"* No. 1641, November 20, 1875:

The Astronomy of the Babylonians.

"The astronomical science of the ancient Babylonians and their pupils, the Assyrians, was neither so profound nor so contemptible as has often been maintained. Now that we are able to read the native records written in the cuneiform or wedge-shaped character, we find that the progress made at a very early period in mapping out the sky, in compiling a calendar, and above all, in observing the phenomena of the heavens, was really wonderful, considering the scanty means they possessed of effecting it. Certainly their astronomy was mixed up with all kinds of astrological absurdities; but this did not prevent them from being persistent and keen observers, whose energy in the cause of knowledge is not undeserving of imitation even in the present day.

"The originators of astronomy in Chaldea, as indeed of all other sciences, art and culture there, were not the Semitic Babylonians, but a people who are now generally termed Accadians, and who spoke an agglutinative language. They had come from the mountains of Elam, or Susiana, on the east, bringing with them the rudiments of writing and civilization. They found a cognate race already settled in Chaldea, and in conjunction with the latter they built the great cities of Babylonia, whose ruins still attest their power and antiquity.

"Somewhere between 3000 and 4000 B. C., the Semites entered the country from the east, and gradually contrived to conquer the whole of it. It is probable the conquest was concluded about 2000 B. C. At all events, Accadian became a dead language two or three centuries later; but as the Semitic invaders owed almost all the civilization they possessed to their more polished predecessors, it remained the language of literature, like Latin in the middle ages, down to the last days of the Assyrian empire.

"Astronomy was included in the branches of science borrowed by the Semitic Babylonians from the Accadians. Consequently their astronomical records contain many words which belong to the old language, while most of the stars bear Accadian and not Semitic names. Even where the Assyrio-Babylonians had a technical term of their own, like *kasritu*, "conjunction," they continued to *write* the old Accadian word *ribanna*, of which *kasritu* was a translation, though they probably pronounced it *kas-ritu*, just as we pronounce *viz.* 'namely.'

"The oldest Chaldean astronomical records of which we know anything are contained in a great work called 'The Observations of Bel,' in seventy books, compiled for a certain king, Sargon of Agané, in Babylonia, before 1700 B. C., and of which we possess later copies or editions, made for the library of Sardanapalus at Nineveh. The catalogue of this work shows that a great part of it was purely astrological; other books, however, were more scientific. Thus, there was one on the conjunction of the sun and moon; another on comets, or, as they are called, 'stars with a corona in front and a tail behind;' a third on the movements of Mars; a fourth on the movements of Venus, and a fifth on the pole star. The catalogue concludes with a curious intimation to the student, who is told to write down the number of the tablet or book he wishes to consult, and the librarian will thereupon hand it to him. The larger portion of the work itself has been recovered, though some of the tablets belonging to it still lie under the soil of Kouyunjik, and a good part of the details which follow is extracted from this primitive Babylonian treatise. The Accadians seem to have begun their astronomical observations before they left Elam, since the meridian was placed in that country, while the old mythology made "the mountain of the east" the pivot on which the sky rested. This will account for the large number of eclipses recorded in the "Observations of Bel," which imply a corresponding antiquity for the commencement of such records. These records were carefully kept, as there were state observatories in most of the Babylonian and Assyrian towns—at Ur, Agané, Nineveh, and Arbela, for instance—and (at all events in later times) the astronomers royal had to send fortnightly reports to the king. It is to the Accadians that we owe both the signs of the zodiac and the days of the week. The heaven was divided into four parts, and the passage of the sun through these marked the four seasons of the year," etc., etc.

A Chronological Table by Different Authors.

The first two follow the Hebrew text, the next three the Septuagint version; Bunsen, neither.

	Usher.	Pelavius.	Hales.	Jackson.	Poole.	Bunsen.	Dynastic.
	B.C.	B.C.	B.C.	B.C.	B.C.	B.C.	B.C.
The Creation of Adam at	4004	3983	5411	5426	5361	20,000	12,500
" Flood,	2348	2327	3155	3170	3099	10,000	4763
" Birth of Abraham,	1921	1961	2078	2043	2157		2000
" Exodus,	1491	1531	1648	1593	1652	1320	
" Building of the Temple,	1012	1012	1027	1014	1011	1004	
" Destruction of the Temple,	588	589	586	586	586	586	
From the Destruction of the Temple to the present year (1876),	years. 2468	years. 2469	years. 2462	years. 2462	years. 2462	years. 2462	years.
Total from Adam to 1876,	5880	5859	7287	7292	7237	21,876	14,376*

* If we add the Hebrew whole numbers in both of the tables of Genesis, and follow Poole's date for the birth of Abraham, we shall have a total of 15,021.

FROM ADAM TO ABRAHAM.

Dates at which different eras begin.

Julian Period,	. 4713 B. C.	Alexandria,	. B. C.	5503
Olympiad, .	. 776 "	Antioch, .	. "	5493
Rome, .	. 753 "	Chinese Cycle, .	"	2277
Jewish, .	. 3761 "	Indian last Kaliyug,	"	3101
First Canicular, .	2785 "	Hegirah, .	. A. D.	622
Constantinople, .	5509 "			

www.ingramcontent.com/pod-product-compliance
Lightning Source LLC
Chambersburg PA
CBHW030248170426
43202CB00009B/669